Published! Now what?

A self-help guidebook for every day writers and artisans

The Rockfish River Valley Short Book Writers Project

Is a mutually beneficial consortium of independent, nonfiction and fiction writers, authors, biographers, essayists, historians, and everyday people who commit to professionally edit and publish local and regional books, using credible printing and publishing platforms to produce high quality paperback books with ISBN and copyright identification.

Wayne H. Drumheller

Copyrighted by Wayne H. Drumheller, 2017
Editor & Founder, The Rockfish River Valley Short Book Writers Project
Celebrating over 200 Authors with Independently Published Books
Printing Platform: Createspace.com
ISBN: 13: 978-1977883209
ISBN: 10: 1977883206

DEDICATION

This book is dedicate to the more than 200 authors with over 300 amazon titles, it has been my pleasure to meet and assist in writing, editing, publishing and selling their books since I founded the self-funded Rockfish River Valley Short Book Writers Project 2010.

This book is also dedicated
to Earl 'John Boy' Hamner, Jr.,
Creator of The Walton's Mountain TV series,
Falcon Crest, Twilight Zone and the animated production of Charlotte's Webb.
He was a Nelson County, Virginia native, who
became a dear friend and mentor to me early in my writing and late in his life.

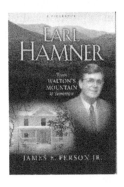

Earl died in Los Angles, California, March 24, 2016. He was 93.

And, my youngest brother, Freddie Rankin Drumheller and my oldest brother, Artie Carroll Drumheller who were friends to many with their stories, tales, adventures and generosity.
Freddie left us much too soon on August 18th, 2018.
Artie left us also, much too soon, on September 18th, 2020
I miss their voices and laughter every day.

Introduction

Published! Now What?

Since I published *Writing As Art, Editing & Publishing* in 2016, I have had many workshop participants and experienced authors ask me this question.

The answer is obvious, but sometimes intimidating. Most of the writers I meet want to write, edit and publish, but do not want to deal with the marketing, sales and the promotions required to be a success as an independently published author. Remember, the simple answer to what's the difference between traditional and independent publishing is not so simple. The simple answer is: traditional publishers are supposed to edit, publish, promote and sell the author's book; versus nontraditional, self or independent publisher who write, edit, publish, promote, market and sell their own books.

As I mentioned in my first book, *Writing as Art, Editing and Publishing*, writing, editing and moving a book toward the publishing and sales point, begins when the author has a printed book proof copy in their hands. Anything before this, such as typed and re-typed revisions, inserted notes, and partial or complete sentence inserts, etc., is still in the artistic or creative phase of writing.

After helping more than 150 aspiring and experienced authors; through more than 85 free workshops in churches, coffee shops and libraries, I still believe writers make a commitment to publish when they print or publish a well-edited proof book. This includes: an illustrated cover, a copyright, title page with ISBN, introduction, dedication, acknowledgement, table of contents, edited contents, and a about the author page, with a correctly formatted back bio cover page for the barcode.

Then, and only then, does a writer start final editing to produce a finished book or novel.

So, very simply, we have the tools to publish today that were out of our reach just 5 years ago. Particularly, independent publishing has had a clear historical path to success beginning with great and well known authors. If we choose, like some before us, to publish and commit to the cost and the specifics of independent-publishing, we can have artistic control and a higher return from our book promotions, signings and sales. It is my hope that the information provided in this book, will give you, the writer and author, useful tools and ideas for promoting, marketing and selling more books.

All the Best

Wayne H. Drumheller,
Editor & Founder
The Creative Short Book Writers Project

ACKNOWLEDGMENTS

I want to acknowledge the authors, bloggers, writers and online editors whose suggestions, opinions and writing platform statements which have included in this book. Their commitment to independent publishing and understanding of the market for selling independent or self-published books is invaluable. I hope the inclusion of their writings receive the respect, recognition and acknowledgement they deserve. I have, to the best of my ability included their contact information when provided.

First, I want to acknowledge Joan Meijer; writecharacter.blogspot.com for her *How to Write An Autobiography That Sells*. She confirms my belief that the first self-published book by an author should be the autobiographic life story. She writes: *"I lecture about writing to non-writers – hypnotists, numerologists, psychics, housewives, businessmen and women and people who often tell me that I should write about them because "they have had very interesting lives."*

I totally agree and thank you Joan for your insights. *Light in the Dark, A Photographer's Story and Portfolio* is seen here from my autobiographical story.

Next, Jane Sutter Brandt leaves her comment on New Tactics: *How to sell out at a book signing without being a celebrity.* As an award-winning journalist with more than 30 years of experience writing, editing, blogging and managing newspapers, magazines, and web sites, she reaches out and gives simple, straight forward advice on hometown book signings. She resides in Rochester, N.Y., where she runs Sutter Communications, which provides a variety of services including writing, editing, public relations, and social media. Her book, *Sutter's Sodas Satisfy: A Memoir of 90 Years of Sutter Drug Co.,* was published in April 2015. For more information visit her blog or Facebook page, or follow her on Twitter. Thanks, Jane.

Alamance County, North Carolina author Carole Troxler, The Red Dog has demonstrated her ability to sign and sell books.

Maeve Maddox, www.dailywritingtips.com presents a look at *Word Count and Book Length*.
The article outlines: "When you are ready to approach an agent or a publisher, study their guidelines carefully and submit your work exactly according to their preferences."
It points out the importance of knowing and following instructions and guidelines.
This may indeed be one most the critical test of success and failure in publishing.
Thank you, Maeve.

Brooke Warner Publisher of *She Writes Press*; President of Warner Coaching Inc.; Author of '*What's Your Book?*' and '*Green-Light Your Book*'. Her *The 10 Biggest Mistakes New Authors Make,* is a must read. Follow Brooke on Twitter: www.twitter.com/brooke_warner. Thank you, Brook.

Rita Odom Mosley's 20,000 word book titled, <u>No School</u> *is destined to be national in sales and outreach.*

Brooke Warner's ***3 Good Reasons to Keep Your Book Shorter than 80,000 Words. Well worth the reading.***

Bidinotto posted *10 Winning Marketing Strategies for Your Self-Published Book* in Book Business, Essays, Wool Bookmark the permalink. This offer hard hitting and straight-forward does and don't in self-publishing, marketing and selling.

Fern Reiss, CEO, PublishingGame.com/Expertizing.com presents a well-rounded publicist approached for children's books with *How to Publicize Your Children's Book.*

Jennifer McCartney's *Indie Success Story: Jen McLaughlin's Shot to the Heart* shows she knew something special was happening with her book the first week after its publication. Follow her at @jennemem.

Categories, genres, and subgenres was posted by CreateSpaceBlogger. (Page 29) Richard Ridley is an award winning author and paid CreateSpace contributor. This article points out that selling is sometimes as simple as knowing what category or genre to focus on.

Maria Murnane, a CreateSpaceBlogger authored *Book marketing tip: Put a sample on Goodreads.* She is a paid CreateSpace contributor and the best-selling author of the *Waverly Bryson series, Cassidy Lane, Katwalk,* and *Wait for the Rain.* She also provides consulting services on book publishing and marketing. Have questions for Maria? You can find her at www.mariamurnane.com.

Marcia Peterson gives us *How to Successfully Market Your Book.* She presents 20 tips and recognizes the tipster with website or blog. She says create some buzz and sell books. She is a columnist for WOW! Women on Writing and the editor of WOW! blog, The Muffin. She lives in Northern California with her husband and two children.

Literary Liaisons: Who's Reading Romance Books? ENTERTAINMENT

Meredith Kaminek wrote *Marketing Self-Published Fine Art Photography Books*. She self-published a book of her fine art photography, together with her own inspirational writings, and then set about publicizing, marketing, and selling her books without the aid of a publisher or publicist.

Alex Palmer penned *Tips for Marketing Self-Published Children's Books and says* marketing self-published children's books requires appealing to both kids and adults.

Lori Welch Wilson is the <u>Tooth Fairy in Disguise</u> and is a master at making public appearance in costume. Her book is a real hit regionally.

Allen Murabayashi wrote an interesting and focused article titled, *Three Approaches to Publishing Your Photo Book*. He is the Chairman and co-founder of **PhotoShelter**, which regularly publishes **resources** for photographers. Allen is a graduate of Yale University, and flosses daily. He offers an encouraging looking at marketing and selling photography books where most authors barely sell 1000 copies.

If you're one of many authors who have self-published a book and you want to get that book into bookstores, have a plan and persevere. And, if you're trouble by the difficulty of getting past the 60 second presentation in brick and mortar book stores, then read the article from amazon; *How to Get a Self-Published Book Into Bookstores*.

Five things your book description says about you is by Bryan Cohen. He says "It's tough to write a 70,000 word book, but it's just as tough to write a book description of a few hundred words." He believes the most important words you write may be part of the simple, emotional, and intriguing description that goes online for all to see. Bryan Cohen is the author of Ted Saves the World, the first book in a YA sci-fi/fantasy series, and a collection of creative writing prompts books. You can find him at www.bryancohen.com.

Bill Tucker's bio for <u>Sad Country Blue</u>, a murder mystery in the Blue Ridge Mountains, shows how important the author's personal life story is to the published book.

13 Reasons why Serials are Better than Books by Molly Barton, co-founder of the new serialized reading experience Serial Box, tells us why original fiction is best digested in episodes.

Marketing Books as an Indie Author is by Doug Dandridge. He is a Florida native, Army veteran and ex-professional college student who spent way too much time in the halls of academia. In December of 2011 he put his first self-publishing efforts online. Since then he had sold over 100,000 copies of his work, and has ranked in the top five on

Amazon Space Opera and Military Science Fiction multiple times. He quit his day job in March 2013, and has since made a successful career as a self-published author.

Paul Jarvis' practical advice in ***Marketing tools for any self-published book*** is so 'practical and useful' that you may want to read it and post it on your office wall.

Self-published romance ebooks top the sales list is an article published about Smashwords' annual ebook survey, and it is quite startling to discover how dominant self-published romance novels have become. In short, the romance genre accounts for a staggering 87% of the top 100 bestsellers on Smashwords and their aggregators.

The Author Bio is an Important Marketing Tool posted by Richard Ridley, CreateSpaceBlogger, suggests that the author biography is oftentimes the last item we think about as self-published authors. Richard Ridley is an award-winning author and paid CreateSpace contributor.

Where and How to Sell Your Poetry Books by Denise Enck looks at what you need to get your work out of those boxes and into the hands of appreciative readers.

How to Pitch And Sell A Movie Based On Your Autobiography Or Life Story by Stephanie Palmer deals with the "my life should be a movie/book" She is the author of the best-selling book Good in a Room. She has helped many writers get agents and managers.

Sexist violence sickens crime critic@byamaliahill-A leading novelist says graphic depictions of sadistic misogyny have become so extreme she refuses to review some new fiction.

How to become an ebook superstar
Ben Galley, a self-published author of fantasy books also offers a consultancy service for would-be writers.

The National book Award
7 Ways to Make a Statement
I Self-Published a Cookbook, Despite It all
How to Leverage Tools on Amazon.com
About the Author

Author's Note:

Let me make the point in this book, just as I did in my first workshop book, *Writing as Art, Editing and Publishing* that there are 'pages, phases and stages' to every published book.

We continue to move through the phases and stages to the heart of the process when the next steps need to be understood---marketing and selling.

The resources in this book cover almost everything I've been asked in my workshops. So, read and learn from some of the experts who have "been there" and succeeded.

All the Best.

Pages, Phases and Stages of Writing a Short Book

This is an outline or guide for a minimum of 126 to 450 plus page books.

Phase 1. Front Cover
Phase 2. Title Page/Copyright/ISBN number
Phase 3. Introduction/Dedication/Acknowledgement
Phase 4. Table of Contents
Phase 5. The Content and Main Body of the Book
Phase 6. Summary, Epilogue, Afterword
Phase 7. Tribute
Phase 8. About the Author
Phase 9. Back Cover/Bio/ Endorsements/Reviews

Wayne's Checklist to Finish and Publish Your Book

Phases of Creating, Editing and Publishing

You are in the Creative Phase if you are:
- ---Writing notes, journaling, revising phrases and sentences, organizing chapters
- ---Gathering photographs, art work, illustrations etc.
- ---Making handwritten notes and inserting ideas into the written or typed page
- ---Sorting, resorting, editing, making and revising the typed manuscript
- ---Waking up at night and revising, rewriting or inserting new ideas or thoughts
- ---Give your typed manuscript to a friend or editor for reading and editing
- ---Self-editing, revising and re-typing your manuscript

You are in the Editing Phase when you:
- ---Make a specific plan for a first proof upload or local printing
- ---Secure a proof reader or editor to edit your proof book copy, or do it yourself
- ---Develop a timeline and date for completion of your book
- ---Reach a confidence point where you are ready order a proof copy
- ---Set up an online or local account with a reputable local printer or publisher
- ---Upload or print your proof hard-book copy for edits and very minor revisions
- ---Make self-edits or minor revisions for second proof copy or secure a proof reader
  or a professional editor to read and edit your proof copy for publication
- ---Set a date for final edits and reviews for a second proof copy or publication
- ---Approve proof book copy for publication, or re-submit for second proof book

You are in the Publishing Phase when you:
- ---Submit an approved proof book copy for final publishing
- ---Outline your personal goals for promotion and sales of your published book
- ---Approve your book for online, local or national distribution
- ---Order a first issue of 20-50 author copies of your book for marketing and sales
- ---Write a local media release and announce the publication and sale of your book
- ---Develop a 10-15 question Q&A about yourself and your book
- ---Secure a presentation and signing event with libraries, coffee shops, book stores, etc
- ---Send email announcements or promote via Facebook or on other social media
- ---Set a goal to market and personally sell 100-250 copies of published book in first 6 months
- ---Follow-up on all activities and announcements

You are in the Publicity, Promotion and Sales Phase when you:
- __ Send out 10-15 media contact letters to local and regional press
- __ Announce signings, zoom presentations and book club events
- __ Have self-directed promotional plan for you published books
- __ Track book sales and royalties on Author Central at KDP.amazon.com
- __ Set up bank account or separate credit card for book sales and publishing cost
- __ Are on track for publishing 2nd, 3rd or more published books

Source: Wayne H. Drumheller...www.waynedrumheller.com...Phone/Text 336-266-6461

What Makes a Book
More Likely to Succeed?
By Brian Jud
brianjud@bookmarketing.com

1. The content has diverse market attraction (mass market appeal; wide acceptability)

2. Broad availability (readily distributable to markets via existing channels)

3. Little or no seasonal variations

4. Customers congregated in market concentrations (segments)

5. A unique point of difference (fills a market need; not a me-too title)

6. Priced competitively and easy to produce at a marketable cost (not a lot of die-cutting, shrink-wrapping of components, etc)

7. Lends itself to existing promotion and advertising techniques

8. Has a low break-even point

9. Suitable for rights sales (foreign, serial, movie)

10. The author has a recognized reputation in the target niche

11. Published with adequate marketing support planned throughout its life cycle

12. Proper implementation of the plan

13. Good production quality

14. Introduced into the right market

15. It has a good title

16. Proper financing. Don't spend so much on production that there is little left   for promotion

17. The author has a long-term perspective

18. Don't rely on distribution channel for selling activities

19. Applicable to sell through retail and non-retail markets

Some editing by author and editor for clarity and regional publishing and marketing appeal.

How to Write An Autobiography That Sells

By Joan Meijer, writecharacter.blogspot.com.

I lecture about writing to non-writers – hypnotists, numerologists, psychics, housewives, businessmen and women and people who often tell me that I should write about them because "they have had very interesting lives." I start my talks with a question. The first question I always ask is, "Who wants to write their autobiography?" About three-quarters of all audiences raise their hands. My next question is, "Can you tell me who will buy your autobiography?" Generally, most of the hands go down, the audience looks uncomfortable and shoulders begin to shrug. That second question is the first question you should ask when considering writing in the area of (auto) biography.

People who get to write autobiographies, or have others write their biographies for them, are men and women who have done something really special in their lives. They were famous movie stars. They were national or international politicians. They were presidents and first ladies. They were incredible fashion designers. They built great dams and bridges. They were successful generals.

Even reaching a high status does not guarantee a biography. William Henry Harrison was only president for 31 days. He did nothing more as president than catch pneumonia at his inauguration and die. So even being president does not guarantee a biography. There are a kazillion generals in history but most of us can count the few we ever heard about without running out of digits. If you want to test that theory Google "Civil War Generals" and see how many there were and how many names you recognize.

Even Custer probably would have been an 'also served' had he not had a last stand.

The first rule of (auto) biography is, "An (auto) biography is not about a person, it is about what a person did." Very often, even if they have had a big career that's not enough. If Audrey Hepburn had been a housewife she would not have generated a biography no matter how gorgeous she was. It is possible that Katharine Hepburn would not have generated a biography without Spencer Tracy.

The second rule of biography addresses the question, "What did the subject of the biography do that would interest an identifiable market that is willing to spend money buying the book?" Books are easier to sell to identified markets than they are to general markets. Even if you have not done something huge in your life, if you have done something small that several thousand people could be expected to want to read about, you can probably get a book published – or sell a self-published book.

Occasionally someone related to a famous person will generate a biography for the famous person, which is really their autobiography that has a large market because of the fame of the parent – particularly if there is a twist to the fame. A case in point was <u>Christina Crawford</u> who wrote "<u>Mommy Dearest</u>." Her mother <u>Joan Crawford</u> was a horrendously abusive mother. In this case the answer to the question "who will buy your book?" is people interested in nasty gossip that will make a relatively famous movie star look really bad. Joan Crawford became less well known for her successful Hollywood career than she was for the harm she did to her daughter. It is quite probable that Joan Crawford would never have been the subject of a biography without that abuse. It is an absolute given that Christina Crawford would not have merited a biography without the abuse by a relatively famous mother.

For years I thought that books were about writing. They are not. They are about selling. 80% of your time as a writer is spent selling your book; selling your book to an agent, selling your book to a publisher, and then selling your book to an identified market. If you don't sell your book, you don't get to quit your day job. It is essential that you identify the people you think you can sell to and allow the interest of your market to inform your writing. Your book comes out of what you know that people like you need or want to know.

Keepin On, Walkin' On
By
Aleen Steinberg

The easiest way to sell your autobiography is to identify a market that wants to read about what you have done, write specifically for that market and find organizations that are interested in that subject that you can use as a venue to sell books to their membership. For example, if your child survived a rare form of cancer you can write about what you did to help that child survive. Write about all the information that you learned during your child's battle against cancer that would be interesting and useful to other families facing a similar battle. The parents of children with cancer, and particularly that form of cancer, are your market. The organizations built around fighting cancer, and particularly that form of cancer, are your marketing venues – the people you talk to, the people you sell your book to. All the things that other parents should know about battling that disease, the way you felt and how you handled your feelings, any techniques that you used to help your child cope with chemo and needles and hospital stays, what you did to help your other children deal with feelings of jealousy and neglect, all that is grist for your mill. What you did, not who you are, is the stuff of (auto) biography.

You can also slide your (auto) biography into "How To" books as part of the introduction that establishes you as an expert in your field. 20 or so pages, about what you learned and how you got to your level of expertise, that inform the reader about why they should read what you have written is your bio-introduction. These biographical chapters often encapsulate the highest and most exciting parts of your life which solves a problem about (auto) biography. Most of us live fairly boring lives with occasional spikes of excitement and activity. Most of us could write an article about the high points of our lives rather than a book. If you turn what you've learned into a "How To" book and talk more about what you can teach and less about yourself and your life, biography is easier to write.

Fictionalizing your biography is another way to write about yourself, interesting episodes in your life and what interests you. In fiction, I generally write in the area of medical thriller or medical rescue. I am a former New York City Paramedic which is a job that can be surprisingly tedious. It is a 'hurry up and wait' profession with a great deal of very dull transport in between a few extremely exciting rescues. In my books I slide in high points from the ambulance. I describe people that I found interesting, situations that fascinated me, amazing accidents and rescues that I participated in or heard about from other Paramedics, techniques that we used in the field, things that we studied that I imagined using in the field. It's not exactly an autobiography, but it pulls from my life, my interests and the lives of those around me. Turning what interests you into fiction increases the amount of material available to you.

Since you may be writing about a field of interest rather than about yourself, you may want to research what has already been written on the subject. Simply because there are other books in your area of expertise does not mean that you should not write in a given area. Think of how many cookbooks there are. What you want to do is read everything that has been written in your area of interest or expertise and figure out what is missing or how you would handle the issue differently. At the very least, you bring yourself and your personal experiences to the table. I wrote a small book called "Date Rape: It's Not Your Fault" which was inspired by my own rape. Are there other books about date rape? Of course there are. But those books did not include my story and how I handled my recovery and they did not reach the same market that I can reach.

To begin the process of writing (auto) biography start by answering the following questions:

* What have you done that other people would be interested in reading about?
* Who would be interested in what you want to write about? - be specific.
* How big is that potential market?
* How do you reach that potential market?
* Check out Facebook, Twitter, Linkedin, Buzz, Yahoo and MySpace to see if there are existing groups that are interested in that subject.
* Are there organizations that might be interested in your subject? If yes, contact them. Become active in them. Become known within them.
* What questions would people who are interested in your subject need or want to know? Make a list of those questions.
* Are there other books on your subject? If there are other books, how would you treat the

subject differently? What information did other authors leave out that you consider important?
* How can you organize your book to stress the differences in what you bring to the table?
These questions should get you started and should lead to other questions that will help you write and organize books about you that will turn you into a successful writer.

Joan Meijer, the oldest daughter of Bonnie Prudden, started writing in the early 1980s in Paramedic trade publications. At that time she had founded The National Emergency Care Advisory Council and was working with network Program Practices Executives to improve representation of emergency care in programming, "Triaging TVs Prehospital Perspective". As a New York City Paramedic she worked downtown New York out of Beekman Downtown Hospital – which served the World Trade Center. During that time she began work on The Character Book her seminal analysis of character which she uses as the background for her blog writecharacter.blogspot.com.

Wayne H. Drumheller's book titled, Light in the Dark, is a fifty-year retrospective of his life as a photojournalist and photographer. It is an expression of his passion to find the best in people through their interaction and contact with events and places. His camera became his sketch pad and his published book gave his journey a lasting legacy of meaning and purpose. Read his autobiographical portfolio and see what he did with his creative talents and skills as a photographer and writer.

Wesley Carter author of Bitter Sweet, How Sweet It Is wrote: "The last thing I want to say, to the readers of this book, is make your life count. Give your time and energy to do something good for someone else. You will be greatly rewarded. Whether you make someone laugh, or smile, or bake homemade cookies for some shut-ins. It will make your day a little brighter."

Keepin' On, Walkin' On is published as a first edition by Aleen Steinberg, Cedar Mountain, NC. She attended the University of Wisconsin before marriage. Her attention and volunteer efforts turned to environmental activism after reading Rachel Carson's Silent Spring. She subsequently helped lead the fight to save both the Green Swamp in Florida and DuPont State Recreational Forest in North Carolina from incompatible development. Aleen currently serves on environmental and philanthropic boards in both Florida and North Carolina. An adventure traveler, she has rafted rivers and climbed mountains on six continents. Living and traveling with indigenous people, she sought and found the humanness, that binds the family of man together.

How to sell out at a book signing without being a celebrity

Guest Columns, NewsTactic. Leave a comment!
When Jane Sutter Brandt told me about her hometown book signing plans when we met for lunch in March, I knew it would be a huge success. I asked her on the spot to write a blog post for us after it happened. Jane is an award-winning journalist with more than 30 years of experience writing, editing, blogging and managing newspapers, magazines, and web sites. She resides in Rochester, N.Y., where she runs Sutter Communications, which provides a variety of services including writing, editing, public relations, and social media. Her book, Sutter's Sodas Satisfy: A Memoir of 90 Years of Sutter Drug Co., *was published in April 2015. For more information visit her blog or Facebook page, or follow her on Twitter.*

By Jane Sutter Brandt

I recently returned to my hometown of Burlington, Iowa, for a signing of my first book, *Sutter's Sodas Satisfy: A Memoir of 90 Years of Sutter Drug Co.*, about my family's business, which existed from 1903-1993.

It was an amazing success: I sold every book that I had with me – all 99 of them. The book store owner ended up taking orders for two dozen more that day.

I must have done something right, *right*?

Book signing success tactics

Here's my to-do list of tactics that contributed to my success:

.

Develop a partnership. Chris Murphy, the owner of my host, Burlington By The Book, alerted the Arts Center of Burlington next door about the signing two months in advance. His enthusiasm was contagious, and Assistant Director Hillaurie Fritz-Bonar came up with the idea to schedule a coordinating event involving "Pop Art" exhibits to draw people downtown to meet up-and-coming artists.

Build excitement in advance on Facebook. Of course, we had a Facebook invitation page and I created a Sutter's Sodas Satisfy Facebook page. But a key to my success was a page called "Pictures of Burlington, Iowa," to which anyone can contribute photos (new and old). While I was writing the book and before the book event, I would post a vintage photo every few weeks. Some of these generated more than 300 likes and more than 100 comments. So, when the book signing came around, people's appetites had already been whetted.

Share part of the book in a blog. My book signing was on May 2 and on March 17; I launched a blog using WordPress. Just like on Facebook, I shared interesting photos with a few paragraphs of information. On the right side of the blog's homepage was information on the book signing. I promoted the blog via Facebook and Twitter.

Plan the book signing as an event. I called it "Sutter Drug Store Homecoming and Book Signing" in press releases and on social media. I invited former employees and patrons to come meet other Sutter family members and reminisce. My mother, sister, and cousin were all there to greet people.

Be diligent about contacting local media well in advance. I mailed press releases with copies of the book about a month before the event. The local newspaper did article with photos on the Sunday before the event (and covered it the day of). In the interest of full disclosure, I was a reporter at that newspaper in the early 1980s but almost none of that staff remain. The local talk radio station did a live interview with me on the Monday before the event.

Appalachian Sunrise

A Photographer's Notebook
By
Wayne Drumheller

I started writing Appalachian Sunrise when I was 17. My plan was to join the army after high school and return home to marry my high school sweetheart. I would get a job at Dupont, build a house in the Blue Ridge Mountains at Nelson County, and live a happy life in the place I had always called home. Life didn't turn out the way I planned. I am a better person for it.

Make the event participatory. I had a poster board on an easel and colored markers and asked attendees to write memories using colored markers. Many did. It's a treasured memento now, which I've shared on Facebook. I asked every person whose book I signed if I could have my photo taken with them. Most said yes and my family took turns shooting photos with their iPhones. (I posted these on Facebook later.) A headshot of my great-grandfather was another prop.

Have promotional materials to give at the event. My budget was limited, so I opted for business-size cards that simply stated the name of the book, my name and phone number, and the URL for the blog. I put a card in each book after I signed it

Carol Taylor, a mother of nine children and a substitute school teacher, found a way to market Lessons in Life *through her personal and group connections in the community. She thought no one would buy her little guidebook for living. But, from a very personable and focused mother of nine, they did. She sold beyond her dreams and goals within the first year. She continues to sell, buy more copies, and sell again.*

Mary Archer and Wayne Drumheller teamed up for a mutually beneficial book signing and placed this 8.5 x 11 Flyer on their table at a local homemade ice cream shop. They met people and sold books.

"Stop By and Introduce Yourself To Us"
The Short Book Writers' Project Presents
Wayne Drumheller, Author, Photojournalist, Local Indie Publisher
"100 BOOKS"
You Ought To Read But Probably Never Will.
Featuring
Mary Archer, Artist, Author, Historian
"Bringing Textile History To Life in Alamance County
Thursday, January 23rd, 2021
4:00-5:00 pm
Hosted By
Smitty's Homemade Ice Cream
107 E. Front Street, Burlington, NC
Receive a $1.00 coupon toward purchase of hot chocolate or ice cream.
Information:waynedrumheller.hd@gmail.com
336-266-6461 phone/text
Sponsored by: Smitty's Homemade Ice Cream and The Short Book Writers Project

Word Count and Book Length

By Maeve Maddox
www.dailywritingtips.com

A novelist of my acquaintance insists that the only way to estimate the number of words in a book is to multiply the number of pages by 250.

That was the formula in the good old days when Courier was the only typeface and typewriters were King.

Now we have computers and word processing software. It's no longer necessary to estimate according to the 250-words-per-page formula. All we have to do is use the WP tool that shows Word Count.

Melanie Dellinger, a 16 year old sophomore, and author of The Burn Nexus and Lillian Cart Ci and the War of Elevens, figured out that 90,000-120,000 words was perfect for her magical fantasy books. She writes, signs and sells locally and regionally. Her third book is in the works.

Publishers want to know the overall length of your book. An approximate word count based on what your WP tells you enable them to estimate costs and other factors involved in printing a book.

Novels for adult readers fall between 80,000 and 120,000 words. A novel of 50,000 would be the absolute minimum for some genres and, unless you are Ken Follett or some other established author, you should view 100,000 as the maximum.

Every genre has its own length preferences. Novels intended for the adult market will be longer than those targeted at children and young adults. A young adult novel will run between 20,000 and 40,000 words. In terms of adult mainstream fiction, that length would be considered a novella.

TIP: Don't compose your novel with skinny margins, single-spacing and some off-the-wall font and then make formatting changes when you're ready to market the completed manuscript.

Draft your novel in standard format from the start:

12-point Times Roman or 12-point Courier.
Double-spacing

Margins set to 1-inch all round
Indented paragraphs

NOTE: Don't put extra spacing between paragraphs unless your intention is to indicate a shift of viewpoint or passage of time.

When you are ready to approach an agent or a publisher, study their guidelines **carefully** and submit your work **exactly** according to their preferences.

The 10 Biggest Mistakes New Authors Make

By Brooke Warner

I have to preface this post by noting how easy it is to make mistakes when you're on the road to becoming a published author. This is an emotional journey, and ego can sometimes get in the way. Then there are the many details you must hold, which even publishers get wrong from time to time. I've experienced firsthand the pain of a few or more projects that went to print with pretty egregious problems. And it hurts. Sometimes entire print runs are destroyed as a result. These top 10 mistakes are among the most common I see in my work with authors. Some are about mindset and others are more technical oversights. If you've made any of these mistakes, you're in good company. The best we can do is learn, and spread the word so others take heed.

1. Believing what they want to hear.

This one's tough to begin with, but writers need to hear it. Many authors get derailed from their projects or coaxed into doing something with their books that goes against their better judgment. This can happen with traditional publishing when an agent or editor tells you to change your project because they're sure they can sell your book. It happens with subsidy publishing companies that try to sell you all sorts of stuff you don't need. At this stage of the game, as hard as it might be, it's time to start to treat your book like a product, not a baby. Having too much emotional attachment can lead to problems.

2. Not taking advantage of every available digital platform.

A lot of authors decide to publish their e-book right out of the gate with Kindle Select, forgoing opportunities to publish on Nook and other digital platforms because they figure all that really matters is Amazon. This is a lost opportunity. If you're publishing traditionally, this one won't apply to you, but no matter how you publish your e-book, publish widely. Especially now, when plenty of readers are choosing not to buy from Amazon.

3. Deciding that they don't need a marketing campaign, or starting one too late.

Marketing starts way before your book is published. Many new authors decide they're not going to market their book, until their book comes out and nothing is happening. It's not selling and they don't know what to do. Then they try to hire a publicist, but it's generally too late. I've worked with a number of women who've had to come around to the idea that they are worthy of spending money on a marketing campaign. These are extra dollars, and the psychological barrier can be high, but really all authors in this day and age — self- or traditionally published — should hire a book publicist.

4. Believing that more is better.

More is not always better, and you want to be careful about what you're signing on for. Many subsidy publishers, for instance, offer publishing packages that include a host of items, which sometimes sound so impressive that you feel like you're getting *A lot* for your money. However, things like your Library of Congress number, your ISBN, or filing your copyright are services that cost the publisher next to nothing. Be wary. I've seen subsidy publishers offering things like book trailers, postcards, and even trips to Book Expo in New York to the tune of thousands of dollars. Don't get stars in your eyes. Use your money wisely and shop around.

5. Going renegade.

This is easy to do. Many authors go renegade because they're trying to save money. They feel that they'll "figure it out" as they make their way through the publishing process. I assure you that going renegade will cost you in the long run. Invest in a single consultation with an expert to better understand your options and what makes sense for you. Be realistic about how much you actually understand about publishing. You don't have to reinvent the wheel. Don't overspend for no good reason (point #4), but don't skimp on getting necessary help, either.

6. Not doing enough research on who they're publishing with.

Many authors just follow ads to a certain publishing solution and stop there. It's important to do due diligence and research. There are thousands of posts online about the difference between KDP. Amazon.com and Ingram Spark, for instance. There are a whole host of partnership publishers (like She Writes Press, Turning Stone Press, and Inkshares) popping up all over the place. Many of them are mission-driven and operate totally outside of the traditional or self-publishing model. Ask for references, and make sure you feel good about the company you're going to be doing business with. You might also want to check the author-advocate site Editors & Predators just to see what's what.

7. Believing that "traditional" is better, no matter what.

This mindset will limit your publishing opportunities. I've seen authors languish for years (literally) in the space of trying to find an agent or waiting for an agent to secure a publishing deal. Traditional publishing is also suffering in two distinct ways: the barriers to entry are so high that it's alienating its base; and it's so focused on author platform and "big books" that it's losing relevance fast. Many more authors than ever before are opting out of traditional publishing for more control and better profit margins on their sales. It's cool to aspire to traditionally publish, but if you're not getting bites, don't let your book die on the shelf just because you harbor some sort of judgment about alternative publishing paths.

8. Failing to get sample product.

If you're going to publish with a hybrid or partnership press, or even if you're going to print your self-published book with CreateSpace, KDP.amazon.com or Ingram Spark, get samples! If the company won't provide them for free, invest the $10 to order one of its books from Amazon. You want to see how the books look and feel. Most authors I work with do not ask for samples, and this is putting a lot of faith into the hands of a company that's producing something so important to you.

9. Not hiring professionals.

A lot of self-published authors skimp on editorial and production, but it's such a bad mistake. Every book should be copyedited and proofread — ideally more than once. There are so many elements to track when it comes to book design, and it's incredibly easy to make mistakes. Over the course of my career as an editor and publisher I've seen all the many mistakes that get caught post-production, and this is with a professional team working on books. Things like running heads, pagination, tables of contents aligned with chapter titles and page numbers — the list goes on and on. Have someone who knows what they're doing review your laid-out pages too. It's crucial to review, review, and review again prior to printing your book.

10. Choosing a print run over print-on-demand (POD).

Some authors should get a print run, but most should not. Unless you absolutely know you can sell 1,000 copies within the first year of publication, don't get a print run. And brace yourself for the fact that selling this many copies is a lot harder to do than you might think. Too many authors naively believe that they will easily sell thousands of copies. I'd urge you to start to consider that selling 1,000 copies as a self-published author constitutes a success. Many of your sales, you must remember, will be e-books. POD is awesome because you only pay for what you sell, so, for the vast majority of you, POD is a smart business decision.

Follow Brooke Warner on Twitter: www.twitter.com/brooke_warner

Brooke Warner Publisher of She Writes Press; President of Warner Coaching Inc.; Author of 'What's Your Book?' and 'Green-Light Your Book'

3 Good Reasons to Keep Your Book Shorter than 80,000 Words

By Brooke Warner

Kill your darlings. It's a phrase you've all heard, but how many of you have been brave enough to be truly ruthless with your own writing, to cut in a big and bold ways when needed? How many of you have written a too-long manuscript and allowed an editor to go in and hack huge swaths of work that represented weeks, maybe months, of effort and tenacity to get on the page? Courageous writers do, but so do writers who understand the business of writing, and why too-long books are more difficult to sell. There are in fact readership, publisher, and cost considerations that factor into why the industry standard for the length of a book is 80,000 words, and I would argue that in today's publishing climate, less is more. Here's why:

1. Attention spans are shorter. People are reading more than ever, but there's more competition than ever for those readers' attention—and not just with other books. As an author you're competing against online content like blogs and news sites, and against anything readers read. If you can, aim for under 80,000 words. I've been working with novelists and memoirists who are writing 60,000-word books, something I would have discouraged ten years ago. Writers will argue with me on this point, I know, reminding me of crazy-long bestsellers (*Goldfinch*, anyone?) and pointing to authors' success with long books (J.K. Rowling, Karl Ove Knausgaard, Ken Follett), but these authors are the exception, and most readers simply don't have the attention span for long narratives. So if you're just starting, aim short; if you're running long and are pre-publication (and you can stomach it), work with an editor to cut cut cut.

2. Overly long books are a red flag to agents and editors. While there will always be space in the literary landscape for authors' magnum opuses, you shouldn't feel that your first book needs to be one. In fact, you're better off if it's not. Putting yourself on the map with something more modest and reasonable is a good strategy. Long books are a big risk, and they're difficult to sell because of agents' and editors' bandwidth. Publishers, for the most part, do not want to grapple with the higher costs of publishing a long book (see point 3), and most authors could use an aggressive edit. Someone recently told me that she thought Jodi Picoult's editor was getting a little soft. I thought this was an interesting observation, but it led me to think about the fact that most editors probably err toward being soft because they're not given the mandate to be aggressive. It's easy to get very precious about your work, and much more difficult to trust that an objective eye (coupled with your hard follow-up work) may be just what your baby needs to truly thrive in the world.

3. The longer the book, the more expensive it is to produce.
Most writers aren't thinking

about the length of their book and its correlation to various expenses, but it's all publishers are thinking about. And if you're self-publishing, or footing your own production or printing bill, you need to be thinking about it too. The longer the book, the more expensive the copyedit, design, and printing. If you have a 400-page book, you're cutting into your profits to keep your price point low. And yet you want to keep the price point competitive to, well, compete. You'll discover if you end up printing your book print on demand (the way of the future) that a single book is expensive, and it behooves you to keep your page count low. The difference in cost between a 60,000- and 100,000-word edit is about 20 hours of work, and about $1.50/unit on printing. So it's a big deal—no matter who's footing the bill.

Do you have a story about having pared down your manuscript that you want to share? Or maybe you have a success story with your long book and you have another angle from which to approach this topic? Either way, I'd love to hear from you.

Follow Brooke Warner on Twitter: www.twitter.com/brooke_warner

Rita Odom Moseley is an African American woman, the older of two children, and was raised in the small Prince Edward County, town of Farmville, where she still resides. She was directly affected as a little girl, along with around 1,700 black schoolmates, by the five-year closing of the public schools in her home town. Her story, and the experience of her schoolmates, is the basis for the book "No School."

Rita Odom Moseley, Community Leader, Historian, Author,
Prince Edward County
Farmville, Virginia   ISBN-13-978-1544940885
81 pages/17.000 words with illustrations

My Black South is a collection of light-hearted vignettes about African-Americans growing up in the south in rural and segregated communities during the 1930s through the 1960s. Some are embellished renditions of stories told and heard. There are many more to be shared. I hope that you enjoy these.

Fran Barry Edwards,
Author, Educator, Humorist
Burlington, NC
ISBN-978-1984263322
107 pages/ 11,000 words with photographs

10 Winning Marketing Strategies for Your Self-Published Book

POSTED BY BIDINOTTO

Some time ago, I published a piece telling aspiring authors **"Ten Reasons You Should Skip Traditional Publishers and Self-Publish Ebooks Instead."** Yet despite the clear advantages of "indie" over "traditional" publishing, the prospect of "DIY" publishing still scares the hell out of many writers. Their most common worry?

- "But…how would I *market* my book on my own?"
- That fear is the main reason why so many hold out forever for a traditional contract, then accept lousy ones. They want a publisher to take the burden of marketing off their backs.
- Well, let me share a dirty little secret that publishers don't want newbie authors to know. Despite all their advance promises to give you lots of promotional support, *they mostly will leave the marketing of your book up to you.*
- That's right: They save their promotional budgets for King, Evanovich, and Grisham—not for struggling beginners or "mid-listers." So, if you'll have to promote your book all by yourself anyway, then why surrender most of your royalties and rights to a publisher?

- Still, the question remains: How *do* you market a self-published book?
- I spent a long time studying the promotional methods of successful self-published authors before I released my debut thriller, *HUNTER*. And, as I have described here, their tips helped *HUNTER* to become a big bestseller in December 2011.

- I learned that becoming a successful "indie" author requires two basic things. First, you must *craft a book that appeals to an identified target audience.* Second, you must *make your book "discoverable" to that target audience.*
- Let me explain what that means, in ten steps:

1. Write the best book you can—then, write your *next* one.

Gerry Kruger wrote her second book: Two of Us: A Father-Daughter Memoir. ISBN- 978-1095577059. She is a teacher, artist, and former NPR Essayist. She lives in Charlottesville, Virginia. Her first book is titled: On Kruger Pond: Charlie's Story. (ISBN- 978-1466345690)

- Crafting an appealing book is 90% of the marketing battle. No amount of marketing ingenuity will help an unappealing book succeed. On the other hand, I've seen great books succeed with little or no marketing push. (Hugh Howey's *Wool* is **an outstanding example.**)
- Bottom line: Good "word-of-mouth" is *the* best advertising.
- In addition to writing *a* good book, the next best marketing tactic is to write *more* good books. Each new title will broaden your name recognition and generate more sales for all your

previous ones. That's because many readers are "binge readers." They find an author they like, and they then seek out and scoop up every single title that the author has written previously.

▪ Even better, write a *series*. Books linked together by some connecting theme (think of John Gray's "Mars and Venus" books), or by some appealing character (think: Harry Potter, Jack Reacher, Stephanie Plum, Tarzan, Sherlock Holmes, Mitch Rapp, Mike Hammer, Scot Harvath, Sean Dillon, Spenser, Elvis Cole, Joe Pike, etc., etc.), will foster a virtual addiction in your fans, who will then eagerly await the publication date for every new installment in the series. Better yet, each new book released will attract new fans, prompting them to go back and buy all the prior books in the series. That's how bestselling authors expand their audience over time, often geometrically.

▪ Every successful author I know agrees: *The* single best "marketing tactic" that you can employ, by far, is to write and publish your next book. In fact, many of them counsel that you shouldn't even bother to begin doing any promotions until you've written and published at least three books. Success in indie publishing is a marathon, not a sprint.

▪ Still, stories of books—especially self-published books—succeeding without *any* marketing, are rare. Most books, even good ones, will languish, invisible among millions of available titles, unless you do something to make them stand out and become visible—*discoverable*—to some target audience.

▪ So, let's assume that you have written a good book. Now, your pre-publication job is to enhance its "discoverability." Here's some key stuff to take care of *before* you publish:

A Blessed Life Together
by Teresa Renee Helt Higgins
"And, we know that in all things God works for the good for those who love him, who have been called according to His purpose." Romans 8:28

▪ **2. Identify your target reader, find out where he is, and think like that reader in every aspect of your marketing.**

▪ No book appeals to everyone. So, don't even try to market broadly and generically; that's a waste of your time and money. Instead…

▪ *1. Narrowly define your target reader audience.* Do they share a demographic profile (age, sex, ethnicity, background, etc.)? What are their values and interests? Who are their heroes? Write a profile of your "ideal reader."

▪ *2. Next, find out where they hang out.* What books and magazines do they read? What movies do they like? What online sites do they frequent? What groups to they belong to? Compile lists of these things; you'll want to target them later.

▪ *3. Now, think like that reader in all aspects of your marketing.* No, this doesn't mean pandering to readers *as a writer.* But in every *marketing* decision and action, ask yourself: *How would this be perceived by my target reader?* Never view marketing decisions as aspects of your artistic self-expression. Marketing is simply the effective communication of values. It means connecting your work with the values and interests of your targeted customer.

3. Don't be amateurish. Be totally professional in all aspects of your writing, editing, and production values.

- Face it: Your book is competing with millions of other titles—many by Big Name authors from major publishers—for the attention, consideration, and purchasing dollars of your target reader. That's why you must give that reader every impression of being as professional as your competitors—and *never* amateurish or "self-published."

- So…*Aim for craftsmanship in your writing*. Always strive to learn and improve. *Be patient*: Take your time to do things right rather than rush to publish. *Test your final manuscript on "beta readers"*: people with writing and editing skills, but especially members of your audience of target readers.

- After their input, *carefully edit, proofread, format, lay out, and design your book*—and preferably, have those tasks done by hired, objective pros. What you may think are "little things"—typos, misspellings, bad punctuation—will be tell-tale signs of "amateur" to many browsing customers, and you'll lose them. Those "little things" count in a big way, if you wish to establish a professional image and reputation. (Here's one place where you can find the good contract help you'll need.)

- *Make sure your cover looks professional*—like a major publisher's. First, it must suggest the right genre to your target reader. Second, it must consist of simple, bold images, and use big, colorful, contemporary fonts for the title and author name. All of this should be visible and legible *when reduced to thumbnail size*, which is how customers will probably first see it online. And third, *test* potential cover designs on some members of your target audience before you decide which to use. Remember: A cover is not about what *you* like; it's about what your *target reader* likes. Don't just grab some images off the Internet; use PhotoShop on them, then select Times Roman fonts for the title and your name. That all-too-common approach simply screams "self-published amateur," and it will turn off many prospective readers. If you're not a graphic designer, spend a couple of hundred bucks and hire one. It will be one of the best investments you'll ever make.

Before I published *HUNTER*, I knew a "noir" look would capture the mood for my vigilante crime thriller. But I needed a cover that would really "pop" and grab the eyes of my target audience from amid the sea of other book covers displayed on sites such as Amazon. My talented young cover designer, Allen Chiu, understood exactly what I was looking for and simply knocked it out of the park. Here is another fundamental consideration for your marketing tactics:

4. Carve out a distinctive market niche, and "brand" yourself and your work. Years ago, I encountered the invaluable little marketing classic by Al Ries and Jack Trout titled *Positioning: The Battle for Your Mind.* Its subtitle is "How to Be Seen and Heard in the Overcrowded Marketplace. "Well, that's what successful indie authors now call "discoverability." And here are a couple of key points about how to enhance it:

- First, *"brand" yourself and your book.* Carve out a narrow, distinctive "niche" in the book marketplace based on some catchy concept, theme, or image that will appeal to your target readers, but simultaneously distinguish your work from all others in your genre.
- Since my novel is about a mysterious vigilante hero, I decided that my brand would be "The Vigilante Author." I use the vigilante concept to distinguish my book from other types of thrillers. But my hero is also distinctive from other fictional vigilante characters, because he's unusually self-reflective and philosophical about what he's doing. In fact, you might describe him as a kind of "philosophical Zorro." So that even more tightly defines my market "niche," setting my work apart.

- Bottom line: Find some catchy, distinctive concept that works for you.

- Second, *use your "brand" in everything you do to promote your work*: book covers, author photos, blog designs, promotional copy, business cards, etc. That kind of focus and integration will guarantee that your "brand" will become uniquely identified with you, making you and your work *memorable* for your target readers.
- You can see by this blog how I employed my "Vigilante Author" brand as its title, then tied the blog's visual theme to my book cover. I even selected an author photo that would reinforce my brand. (And yeah, I wear that "Indiana Jones" hat in public a lot. Besides good branding, I think it just looks cool. And I'm old enough not to care if anyone thinks otherwise.)

5. Don't price your book either too low or too high. Price it strategically to be competitive.
- Some indie authors have achieved a lot of success by running temporary sales on their ebooks—even setting the price at "free" for a few days. This tactic can generate a lot of visibility and build your fan base quickly. Applied to one book in an ongoing series, low or free pricing also can attract many readers who'll then go and buy all the others.

- But obviously, it's not a great tactic to give away your work permanently, not if your long-term goal is to make writing books a paying proposition.

- So again: "Think like your target reader." If you price your ebook too low—say, 99 cents—he may think: "Cheap—probably self-published—probably lousy quality." On the other hand, if you price it too high, you'll lose a lot of sales because you aren't a household name like King or Clancy or Evanovich.

- You also should know that ebook pricing affects royalties. On Amazon, for example, you get 35% royalties on ebooks priced from 99 cents up to $2.98, 70% on ebooks priced between $2.99 and $9.99, and then back down to 35% on books priced at $10 or higher. Clearly, you make the most money per sale by pricing between $2.99 and $9.99.

- Personally, I think the pricing "sweet spot" for ebooks by a newbie, self-published author lies between $2.99 – $4.99 for a full-length ebook, around $1.99 for an e-published novella, and 99 cents to $1.99 for an e-edition of a short story. (FYI: I priced *HUNTER* at $3.99 from the outset and I've never regretted that decision.)

▪ After you've earned a Big Name, you can and probably should raise your prices. But I wouldn't try doing that until I had an established following and multiple titles.

▪ For print editions, I think you should try to price your book just a bit lower than comparable hardcovers or paperbacks issued by major publishers—again, until you acquire a good fan base.

▪ Now, I want to mention one of the most important, yet neglected things that an author can do to generate sales:

6. Don't be dull! Carefully craft compelling promotional copy on your Amazon, Barnes & Noble, and other online product pages. This is one of the biggest failings of most self-published authors. They knock themselves out parsing every sentence inside their book—yet they treat what they say *about* their book, in its product descriptions and marketing materials, as an afterthought. Many of their book blurbs are about as exciting as cooking recipes. And then they wonder why their books don't sell.
▪ You must craft *compelling product descriptions, with endorsement blurbs* (if you have them), for your product pages on Amazon and elsewhere. Because most prospective buyers eventually will wind up on online product sales pages, your product description will be your book's final sales pitch. Its only purpose is to "close the sale." So, make sure it is as colorful and persuasive as possible.
▪ Study the dust-jacket copy of books issued by major publishers in your genre, just to get a feel for the style, cadence, and layout of riveting promotional copy. *That* is what you're looking to emulate.
▪ Then test some drafts of your blurbs on members of your target audience and see what language grabs them. If your description arouses just enough interest and intrigue to prompt a purchase, that's good enough.

▪ And remember: Promotional copy is supposed to be only a *teaser*—not an exhaustive presentation of the story. Its job is to build curiosity, not to satisfy it. You build intense curiosity not by revealing everything, but by what you *don't* reveal.

▪ Then, there are tactics you can employ specifically on Amazon to attract readers:

7. Make it *easy* for your target readers to find your book by categorizing it *strategically* on Amazon.
▪ Amazon is the 800-pound gorilla of online book marketing. To help readers find the books they like, Amazon provides a host of book categories and subcategories, distinguished by genres and subgenres, each with its own bestseller list.
▪ This will help your target reader find *your* title—but only if you've categorized it in the places where he most likely will be searching for your kind of book. In addition, if you can get your book to show up prominently on some Amazon subcategory bestseller list, it will further boost its visibility to readers.
▪ So, how do you do this? When you first publish your book, Amazon allows you to list it in two separate categories or subcategories. But to make it easier to discover, don't just list it in the

broadest, most generic categories, like "Romance" or "Mysteries" or "Thrillers." Dig down into the less-populated subcategories with fewer titles (e.g., "Romantic Suspense," "Technothrillers," "British Mysteries"), where your book will stand out better.

- You want to choose subcategories that, first of all, are most likely to be searched by your target reader. But then, to make it easier for your book to get onto some subcategory bestseller lists, pick appropriate subgenres *with the fewest competing titles.* You can find out exactly how many books are listed in each genre category and subcategory by searching the category "tree" on the left side of many Amazon book listing pages. And if you have trouble listing your book in the subcategories you want, just email Amazon. Their staff will be more than willing to help you.
- There are also some things that you should (and shouldn't) do in order to build a loyal readership.

8. Don't become a "book-spammer." Instead, establish personal, helpful, mutually rewarding relationships with your readers.

- Many successful self-publishing authors are convinced that paid ads are usually a waste of money. I agree.

- I also think that many self-publishing authors are inept when it comes to using social media. They send out constant email blasts and Tweets about their books, becoming pests. That's because they approach social relationships as "takers" rather than "traders."
- A trader knows that if you want to get something from someone, you have to give back something in return.

- The most cost-effective promotion and marketing strategy is to *befriend your readers via online social networking.* Don't run yourself ragged doing this. I recommend that you pick a single online networking or discussion site, either Facebook, Google +, Goodreads, or Twitter. Become a valuable contributor there. Also, you might occasionally join in on blogs and discussion forums in your book's genre or topical area(s) of interest. That's where your target readers are likely to be. Hang out in those places mainly to make friends and learn, and you'll occasionally find natural, unobtrusive ways to mention your book(s) and generate curiosity. Again, just don't overdo the self-promotion.
- *Establish an author's blog/website.* Write about interesting stuff related to your book's subject matter—but not about the book itself all the time. You might interview other indie authors in your genre; some will return the favor. You also can ask book bloggers and fellow authors to review your books. Some will. **Here** are **a few** highly regarded **blogs** hosted by **several** super-successful **indie authors**. Study what they do and ask yourself why it works.
- *Contact groups and publications that share your interests* and/or an interest in your book's subject matter, and look for opportunities for cross-promotion.
- *Approach your local newspaper(s)*, both in your current area and where you grew up; they love to publish "local boy/girl makes good" features. Libraries, book clubs, and civic groups also like to host local authors.

- *Buy and use business cards that feature your book.* You can design your own high-quality business cards and get them dirt cheap on sites like **GotPrint.com**. As for how to design and use them effectively, check out publisher **Robin Sullivan's excellent advice.**
- *Answer all email and blog comments from your readers*, and compile an email contact list of fans. This is very important: You can use that list to announce and promote your subsequent books to them, and that will give your next title a good crack at the bestseller lists on its publication date.
- As you build authentic relationships and friendships with your readers, you can engage with them further in order to help you succeed:

9. Encourage satisfied readers to leave reviews of your book on Amazon.

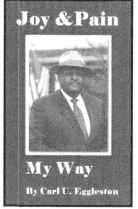

- *The* best advertising is "word of mouth" from satisfied customers. When enthusiastic fans contact you, ask them to consider posting "reader reviews" at your book's product pages on Amazon, Barnes & Noble, Smashwords, Goodreads, etc.Their affirmation of your book's worth will reassure browsing customers and persuade many to give it a chance.
- *However*, don't go out and *actively solicit* reviews from friends and relatives, and never post *fake* reviews or use any deceptive methods to try to "game the system." Don't try to artificially inflate your book's ratings by conspiring with fellow indie authors to post mutually flattering "customer reviews." These tactics only devalue the worth of reviews and hurt you and all indie authors in the long run.
- There's a final thing I recommend, again based on personal experience:

10. Utilize Amazon's marketing tools.

For the foreseeable future, Amazon remains your best bet for attaining self-publishing success. And it provides a host of tools for indie authors to maximize their visibility and reach. Here are a few specific ways to utilize those tools to your advantage:

- *Participate in special promotions, if invited.* I speak from experience. Based on my book's good reviews and steady sales, Amazon invited me to participate in one such week-long promotion late last November. Over the next 35 days, I sold over 50,000 copies of *HUNTER*.
- *Exploit your ranking on category bestseller lists in your promotions.* If you've hit some subcategory bestseller list, use that fact in your marketing blurbs and product descriptions. Don't be modest. Remember what the early baseball great "Dizzy" Dean said: "Ya ain't braggin' if ya can back it up."
- *Consider opportunities to run short-term "free" giveaways and promotions for your ebook.* I've mentioned this earlier. I should add that I haven't yet done this myself, but it does work for some authors.

Don't panic if your book doesn't sell right away.

▪   These tips barely scratch the surface of the many methods you can employ to market your books effectively. But they're a good beginning.

▪   However, don't panic if they don't work to produce stellar sales immediately.

▪   Remember: *Ebooks are forever.* Once available online, your ebook (or print-on-demand book) isn't going to go away. It can sit there on a server indefinitely while you continue to experiment with its cover, your promotional blurbs, your marketing campaign…even its *content.* Yes, unlike a book released by a traditional publisher, you can go back and fix things you don't like. Eventually, if it's an appealing book, it *will* find its audience.

▪   Meanwhile, as you wait for that to happen, let me repeat that *the* smartest marketing move you can make, bar none, is to start writing your next book.

▪   And if you're still not convinced that self-publishing is the right route for you, read or reread **my earlier post** on that topic.

▪   Good luck, and happy writing!

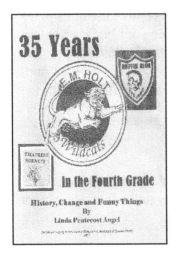

35 Years in the Fourth Grade was written By Linda Angel who is a native of Alamance County, Graham, NC. She was given a box of handwritten poems twenty-years ago that her maternal grandmother had written. Not being a typist, she slowly and lovingly typed the poems to honor her grandmother. They never sold very well so she wrote her second book: **35 Years in the Fourth Grade** It is a treasure chest of memories, photographs and school children's thoughts and mementos. It can become a local best seller to former students and their children. It is destined to become a much sought after book for those who know Linda.

This entry was posted in Book business, Essays, HUNTER: A Thriller, Marketing Advice, Publishing Advice, Self-Publishing, Writing Advice and tagged Al Ries, Amazon, Amazon categories, Amazon Kindle self-publishing, author branding, authors, Bidinotto, Bob Mayer, book genres, book marketing, book niche marketing, book promotion, branding books, CJ Lyons, Dean Wesley Smith, Dylan Hunter, ebook genres, ebook pricing, Elvis Cole, Hugh Howey, HUNTER: A Thriller, indie authors, indie publishing, Jack Reacher, Jack Trout, Joe Konrath, Joe Pike, John Gray, Kristine Katherine Rusch, marketing ebooks, Mike Hammer, Mitch Rapp, Positioning, print on demand, Robert Bidinotto, Scot Harvath, self-publishing, Sherlock Holmes, Spenser, Stephanie Plum, Tarzan, vigilante author, Wool. Bookmark the permalink.

How to Publicize Your Children's Book

by Fern Reiss, CEO, PublishingGame.com/Expertizing.com

How do you publicize a children's book? Many authors of children's books don't spend much time trying—but publicizing a children's book can be easier than publicizing an adult novel. Here's how to get started:

Offer a fan club

Initiate a fan club based on your children's book. Do monthly or quarterly mailings of educational material related to your book topic, or 'news' about the book or characters. You can even consider offering t-shirts, totes, and hats as part of the club's benefits; each of these can be imprinted with slogans or illustrations from the book. You can set this up easily with no monetary investment at Café Press; see www.CafePress.com/publishinggame to look at our example.

Don't forget the online component

Even young children are using the World-Wide Web today. A website for your fans—with information about the book, its characters, side stories about characters from the book, prologues or epilogues, a place for your fans to chat about your book—can help boost interest in your book.

Figure out a reading alternative

Sadly, not that many people attend book readings, even of children's books, unless the author is already famous. So what can you do if you're a good, but not-yet-famous writer? Design an alternative to the traditional reading. Your target audience (and their parents) will be interested in a nonfiction presentation or event just as much (or maybe more) than a reading—and you'll likely sell more books as a result.

Do an event

Do a bookstore demonstration instead of a reading. If your book features an acrobat, design a gymnastics event; maybe you could even organize a gymnastics marathon as a charity event. If your book involves a child who cooks, put together a kids' cooking demonstration. If you have a book about animals, consider organizing a petting zoo.

Do a dramatization or a game

Children's mystery writers can create children-participation mystery programs, featuring the book's characters. Children's science fiction writers could do a presentation on how the 'fiction' in kids' science fiction is based on today's scientific reality.

Every child would consider himself lucky to be featured by name in a children's book!

Go in character

Try going on radio shows and talk shows **in character** – and see what kind of response you get. No one does this—but someone should. Or walk around a busy resort town dressed as a character from your children's book. Better yet, get a few kids to accompany you. Hand out promotional postcards or bookmarks with cute words of wisdom from the book. Remember—in promoting children's books, as in promoting anything else, put something **useful** on the back of any postcard, bookmark, or flyer you produce, so that people will keep your material.

Implement any one of these ideas—and watch your children's book sales take off.

(Interested in learning more about publicizing your children's book? Find out more at www.PublishingGame.com/childrenreport.htm.)

Fern Reiss is CEO of PublishingGame.com (www.PublishingGame.com) and Expertizing.com (www.Expertizing.com) and the author of the books, *The Publishing Game: Find an Agent in 30 Days, The Publishing Game: Bestseller in 30 Days*, and *The Publishing Game: Publish a Book in 30 Days* as well as several other award-winning books. She is also the Director of the International Association of Writers (www.AssociationofWriters.com) providing publicity vehicles to writers worldwide. She also runs The Expertizing® Publicity Forum where you can pitch your book or business directly to journalists; more information at www.Expertizing.com/forum.htm. Sign up for her complimentary newsletter at www.PublishingGame.com/signup.htm.

Copyright © 2011 Fern Reiss

Illustration is cover of "Tooth Fairy in Disguise". The author in costume is Lori Welch Wilson from Yanceyville, North Carolina. Buy her book and read about how her childhood dream become a reality and positive children's book about the healthy benefit of good dental health.

Indie Success Story:
Jen McLaughlin's Shot to the Heart

Self-published author hits the mark with military romance

By Jennifer McCartney

Jen McLaughlin knew something special was happening with her book the first week after its publication.

"I'm very slow to get excited about things. Once I hit [*The New York Times* bestseller] list I had to sit down for a minute," says the indie author. McLaughlin's first self-published romance novel, *Out of Line*, went on to sell over 150,000 copies and hit number nine on *The Times* e-book bestseller list, number 16 on *The Times* combined e-book and print bestseller list, number 28 on the *USA Today* bestseller list, and number one in Amazon's Contemporary Romance category. It's the kind of success that indie authors dream about -- but it didn't happen without a lot of hard work.

While McLaughlin has had previous success publishing with e-publisher Entangled under the name Diane Alberts, she wanted to try her hand at writing a new adult military romance and "just had a feeling that self-publishing was the way to go." Publishing both with a traditional digital publisher and as an indie author, she considers herself a hybrid. "I think it's good to have your name in different places," she says.

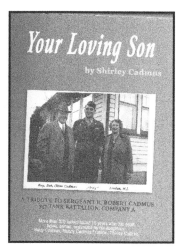

Once she'd decided to go the indie route, she took the publishing process seriously and hired an editor, a cover designer, and a publicist. "It paid off," McLaughlin says. "I wasn't going to put out a book that was mediocre."

Finding an Audience

McLaughlin's Out of Line series (which now includes *Out of Line, Out of Time*, and *Out of Mind*) began with her belief that there was a gap between the kinds of romance books that were being published and the kind she herself would want to read -- a gap she felt she could help to fill. The married mother of four had been writing contemporary romance for two years as Diane Alberts and had published 18 books since the release of her first, *Kill Me Tomorrow*, in October of 2011.

But in 2013, the Pennsylvania-based author wanted to try something new and she decided to try writing under her own name for a new adult audience -- a quickly growing category that straddles the line between young adult and adult fiction and usually features characters in their late teens or early 20s.

Over 2 million American soldiers have served the United States in both Iraq and Afghanistan, so McLaughlin felt there was a large audience of younger women -- first and foremost the wives and girlfriends of veterans -- who would want to read about what it was like to date, fall in love, or be married to someone who had served overseas.

As a result of the younger age group she was trying to reach, she says "I was nervous of how steamy to make it. But you don't have to dumb it down. [The readers] like steamy." She wrote the book with the same level of sex that she includes in her adult titles -- although she does post a warning to potential readers that the series contains adult content and advises readers that they should be over 17 to read her books.

The first book in the Out of Line series and the book that catapulted McLaughlin onto the bestseller lists features Carrie, a senator's daughter, who is off to college in California and just wants to be a normal girl living her life without a bodyguard. Unbeknownst to Carrie, her father enlists US Marine (and avid surfer) Finn Coram to watch out for her -- and they fall in love. When she finds out who he really is "all hell breaks loose," says McLaughlin.

From Rescue Dog to Therapy Dog
Ginger's Journey
By
Shirley Sanders, Ph.D.

It was a "new and novel idea" and she had a feeling it might do well. But first, McLaughlin needed to make sure she went about self-publishing the book in a professional manner. Once the manuscript for *Out of Line* was completed she plotted her next steps.

Preparing to Launch

While there's no guaranteed formula for creating a bestseller, McLaughlin says her indie-publishing success required the following components: "Good writing, good editing, followed by a pretty cover, followed by publicity."

Step One: Hire an Editor

To help edit the book she enlisted the services of a content editor at Coat of Polish Edits who helped her to shape the narrative and fine tune the plot. Next, she hired a copy editor. Readers who review on Amazon, Goodreads, or their own blogs, expect to have a clean reading experience when they purchase an e-book and finding one too many typos or grammatical errors can earn an author a bad review -- whether the reader enjoyed the plot and characters or not.

"If you're going to [be an indie author] make sure that you hire editors," McLaughlin says.

Step Two: Hire a Designer

Once the editorial process was complete, she concentrated on the design of the interior and cover. E.M. Tippets Book Design typeset the manuscript, and cover artist Sarah Hansen at Okay Creations designed a cover in keeping with the romance genre. The final design features a bold title treatment in crimson along with a photograph of a reclining long-haired woman and a young, clean-cut man locked in an embrace.

Step Three: Hire a Publicist

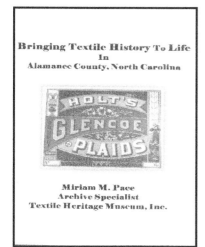

Bringing Textile History To Life
In
Alamance County, North Carolina

HOLT'S GLENCOE PLAIDS

Miriam M. Pace
Archive Specialist
Textile Heritage Museum, Inc.

The last step in McLaughlin's plan was to hire the literary publicity firm InkSlinger. To help McLaughlin attract media attention for *Out of Line*, InkSlinger offered publicity services such as press releases, blog tours, and book signings. Working with publicist Jessica Estep (a former publicist with Entangled Publishing) they began by setting up a Goodreads contest a few weeks before the September 2013 publication date. Over 1,000 readers added the book to their "to-read" shelf in the lead up to publication, and seven months after publication *Out of Line* has close to 4,000 ratings on Goodreads.

Author Miriam M. Pace, Archive Specialist, and her book designer and art illustrator, Mary M. Archer present an interesting sampling of history. What could have been relegated to the dust bins of history is now alive and well at the museum at Glencoe, N.C.

McLaughlin and Estep also set up a "publicity blitz," rallying readers to sign up on the author's website and win a bonus scene from the book by participating in a social media campaign. Estep also planned a blog tour that would commence as soon as the book published. McLaughlin secured a blurb from *New York Times* bestselling author Monica Murphy for the cover. "We had a huge cover reveal," recalls McLaughlin. "There was a lot of interest in it immediately."

All told, McLaughlin estimates she invested about $1,200 of her own money to publish and publicize her book. She admits it was a team effort. "I don't really consider myself self-published," McLaughlin says. "I have so many people helping me."

After conferring with her agent, Louise Fury of the Bent Agency, McLaughlin decided to release the book across all e-book platforms at once. They also decided to price the book at 99 cents for the first week before raising it to the current price of $2.99. McLaughlin figured the downside to a low price point was minimal. "What do I have to lose, so why not? It came out very strong," she says. She spent the first few days watching the Amazon ranking climb towards number one in its category. "I would text my agent the numbers. She said I was going to hit the [*New York Times* bestseller] list." It was her first book as a new adult author and after its immediate success she quickly published the second book in the series to keep the momentum going.

Capitalizing on the Success of an Indie E-Book

Unlike traditional publishing where an author must often wait over a year to see her book published, McLaughlin was able to keep control of the publishing schedule and release the next book in the series just months after *Out of Line* was published. *Out of Time* was released in December 2013 and *Out of Mind*, the third title, publishes in April of 2014. McLaughlin is following the same editing, design, and publicity plan as she did for her first two titles. The third book explores the challenges that many couples face in attempting to have a normal, healthy relationship when one partner is a veteran who suffers from Post-Traumatic Stress Disorder. "My goal all along was to show how Marines change over time," McLaughlin explains. "They go over there and they come home and have to deal with what they've seen and blend in when they get home." With an estimated one in five veterans returning from war suffering from some form of PTSD, it's a message McLaughlin hopes will resonate with her existing readers and also one that might attract a new audience.

At the end of March, McLaughlin's agent concluded a deal with Italian publisher Newton Compton for print and digital rights to all three books in the Out Of Line series. She acknowledges that foreign rights deals for indie authors are rare and is thrilled with the development. "We've kept our options open for print," McLaughlin says. "If it was the right offer [from a traditional publisher] then absolutely."

Jennifer McCartney is an author and editor. Follow her at @jennemem.

Categories, genres, and subgenres

Posted by CreateSpaceBlogger

When it comes to marketing, you're going to want to nail down the genre of your book as soon as you can. Yes, I know most authors know the genre before they even start writing, but a surprising number of authors reject the notion of genre fiction. Most do it as a misguided artistic choice, but some do it because they don't want to limit their reading audience.

By choosing a genre, you're not limiting your reading audience, you're identifying them. My suggestion is to dive deeper and select your sub-genre categories. The more specific you can get the more likely it is that you are going to be able to locate your readers and market to them more effectively.

One of my books falls under the following category, genres, and sub-genre: Teen and Young Adult -- Horror -- Science Fiction and Fantasy -- Science Fiction -- Post-Apocalyptic.

Now, I have been contacted by many adult readers who've expressed that they enjoyed the book, so you may think that by putting the book in the Teen and Young Adult category that I am limiting my reach with a potential pool of readers. But in reality, there is a segment of adult readers that seek out Teen and Adult books. However, conversely, the segment of teen and young adult readers seeking out adult market books is much smaller. So, the smarter play here is to categorize it in the Teen and Young Adult market where I will reach a majority of interested readers.

Categories, genres, and subgenres, weren't invented by retailers to help them organize their titles. They were invented by publishers to help them market their books.
Know your genre and you know your reader.

-Richard Ridley is an award winning author and paid CreateSpace contributor

Book marketing tip: Put a sample on Goodreads

Posted by CreateSpaceBlogger

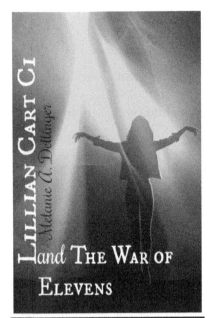

Letters to My Father in Law
Whom I have never met
By
Julia C. Huneycutt

I was recently playing around with my Goodreads profile to update it with my latest novel when I saw an "add preview" option underneath each of my books. I don't know if this is a new feature or one I simply never noticed, but I quickly took advantage of it! Here's how it works:

When you log into Goodreads.com, on the top right corner of the home page you will see your photo. (If you don't have a Goodreads profile, make one now!)

If you click on your photo, the drop-down menu will include "author dashboard."

Go into your author dashboard, and you will see your book(s), the number of reviews, etc.

Underneath each title you will see the "add preview" option. Click on the "add preview" button and follow the instructions to upload a sample. (What you upload is up to you. For my books I chose the prologue, or the first chapter if there is no prologue.)

That's it! Now when people visit my profile page or come across the detail page of any of my books, they will be able to open a sample chapter just by clicking on a button that says "preview."

Isn't that cool? Just like giving free tastes at an ice cream shop, offering readers a free glimpse of your writing is a great way to draw them in. If they enjoy the sample, chances are they're going to want to keep reading and will be willing to pay to do it. That translates into a sale for you, as well as a potential new fan!

-Maria Murnane is a paid CreateSpace contributor and the best-selling author of the Waverly Bryson series, Cassidy Lane, Katwalk, and Wait for the Rain. *She also provides consulting services on book publishing and marketing. Have questions for Maria? You can find her* at *www.mariamurnane.com.*

How to Successfully Market Your Book

By Marcia Peterson

How do you promote your book?

As an author, writing your book and getting it published are just the beginning of the process. You also need to get your book into the hands of as many readers as possible. So, what things should you be doing to promote your work and sell as many book copies as possible?

Luckily, writers are a generous bunch, and many were willing to share their secrets, author-to-author. We chose the most useful, innovative, and doable marketing ideas that they revealed to us and we offer them below for your benefit. From press releases and podcast interviews to a few interesting ways of using Facebook and other online tools (plus so much more!), these authors tell you how to make your book known.

Whether you have a little help from your publisher or not, there's so much you can do. Take a look at all the great ideas, and dedicate yourself to the promotion strategies that seem like a fit for you and your book. Have fun, and sell books!

1. **Make news.** The publication of a book isn't news anymore. That's why I suggest creating a buzz around the theme of your book and telling the press about it. For example, if your novel features a homeless couple, develop a program to help local homeless people. Serve sandwiches or a hot meal in the park every Sunday, for example. For a book on family budgeting, offer free classes through local churches for those who are struggling financially. Perhaps your children's book focuses on personal hygiene for kids. Solicit local dentists to offer free exams for kids once a month and entertain kids who are waiting by reading your book to them. Contact local newspapers with your "breaking news" and be sure to mention your book in the interview.
-Patricia Fry
www.matilijapress.com/PromoteYourBook.html

2. **When _The Whole Package_ (Penguin-Berkley, 2011) hit the shelves**, I knew the real work had just started. One of the most effective ways I got the word out was through Facebook. I wrote a brief letter to each one of my friends, asking them to post a link about the book on their wall. The response was overwhelming! Not only did people help spread the word, they asked people to buy it! I was stunned to watch *The Whole Package* shoot to the top of the online charts, thanks to a little—okay, a lot!—of help from my friends.
-Cynthia Ellingsen
www.cynthiaellingsen.com

3. **If you are a COSTCO member**, e-mail their *Connection* magazine, sending a few paragraphs describing your book (topic, target audience, why it would interest or help people, what led you to write it). They often include these vignettes about what their members are doing on their "Member Connection" page. I did so for a book I wrote with my young daughter (*The Braces Cookbook: Recipes You (and Your Orthodontist) Will Love*). I sold more than three hundred copies in one month because of that article, even though COSTCO did not carry the book in its stores. It also made a great clipping (copied in color) to add to my article/review portfolio.
-Pamela Waterman
www.MetalMouthMedia.net

4. **Turn one of the best excerpts from your book** into a blog/website post. At the end of the post, provide a link where readers can order the book. This works wonders for me, especially when I can tie the excerpt to a news hook.
-Laura Shumaker
www.laurashumaker.com

5. **Author video on your home page moves** you up dramatically in search engines. People get to "meet you" and discover "what your book can do for them."
Blog, blog, blog—and comment on blogs. Create those backlinks with keywords to make your author site stand out on search engines. *Walking on Sunshine* appears on the second page of a key word search for "grief." Enter contests and awards. Having someone validate your book as above the curve with an award instills curiosity and interest. It also moves your book up on displays—front cover vs. spine.
-Sheryl Hill
www.walkingonsunshine.org

6. **Find podcasts who need guests.** While you might not be able to get on *Oprah*, you can get on a wide variety of podcasts. And the good news is most podcasts are looking for interesting guests. So develop a guest pitch, make a list of podcasts you think might be interested in your story, and contact them about possibly being a guest. Give them a free copy of your book to read in e-book form; and if they like your book, they will basically sell it for you. Most of my sales have come from podcast interviews.
-Jen Hancock
www.jen-hancock.com

7. **Don't just go after the national or mainstream magazines,** TV stations, or newspapers. I would focus on the local angle by contacting, for TV, all of the local news channels—first in your town, then city, and then state. When you get a couple local appearances, then use those clips to pitch bigger outlets.
-Natasha Burton
www.bigredflags.com

8. **If you've previously only thought about Amazon.com as a 24/7 virtual bookstore**, think again. Features such as "So You'd Like To...Guides" and "Listmania"—as well as regular participation in online discussion groups—will establish you as an expert in your field. Use "Inside the Book" as a teaser to reel in readers. And don't forget that

clubs and schools are always seeking guest speakers for meetings, special events, and "career day." They'll welcome the addition of your name—a local success story—on their rosters! Too shy to talk? Let technology be your voice by sharing your views and building a network through social media channels such as Facebook, Twitter, LinkedIn, American Chronicle, Gather, The Red Room, and NovelSpot. Start a ripple, create some waves, and employ all the imagination and tenacity that you can to make your new book the splashing success it deserves to be.

-Christina Hamlett
www.authorhamlett.com

9. **Make the web your marketing tool**. Dedicate one hour every day—seven days a week—to use blogs in your area of interest. Offer free samples for other bloggers to review. Offer to review their work. Offer to write a guest blog. Mention them on your blog.

At holiday time, see if you can tie your book in with the holiday—if it's a romance, hit hard before Valentine's Day. If it's got strong African-American content, hit hard for Martin Luther King's birthday weekend. Read HARO and other sites seeking author info, and answer as many as you can to build up your web presence and recognition factor. Be a guest speaker on topics in your book on blog talk radio stations; then use that experience to get onto local stations. Offer yourself as a backup for a last minute fallout for a talk show.

-Francine L. Trevens
www.writerfrancinetrevens.co

10. **My "secret weapon" is <u>Vistaprint</u>.** They can produce many great promotional marketing tools for your books, and many of them for FREE. For example, I get postcards, letterhead, notepads, notecards, t-shirts, magnets, you name it—in minute, small orders—all geared to my book, and most of them for FREE. My book is the world's first beauty book for traveling women; and when I am at the airport, I personally hand out my postcards about my book to all of the flight attendants I come in contact with. Usually, promotional products companies require that you make huge purchases, and so Vistaprint is ideal for the author. I also use the letterhead, labels, etc. when I send out my book to the media. And all are custom designed by me with all of my personal images that I upload.

-Debbi Karpowicz Kickham
www.GorgeousGlobetrotter.com

11. **If you plan on speaking** within your industry field due to your book, you need to begin the process in advance. If your book will be published in August, let's say, you should have already put together a list of potential targets for speaking at conventions, bookstores, etc. for the upcoming year. Plan your own book tour, and your publicity and sales will be much better than just sending out a press release. I booked my own book tour, which included visiting more than fifty cities and over thirty speaking engagements; and each provided a publicity opportunity to promote the book and book signings.

-Linda Duke www.marketing-cookbook.com

12. There's always discussion amongst authors about ways to promote their books. People get caught up in blogs, Facebook author pages, Twitter posts, forums, etc., etc. and forget about press releases. Only you can determine who should get your press release, depending on your demographic, subject matter, location, etc. Make sure you send these e-mails individually and not in a group blast. Today's press really wants short and sweet press releases. They want the information to the point—no more than a few paragraphs. And attach your cover art in a small jpg. Don't clog their in-boxes. Many newspapers and media outlets are short-staffed. If your release is too long, they won't take the time to read it. A lot of section editors will just paraphrase your release into a few short sentences and put it in the "Notes" section. Press is press—be happy.
-K. S. Brooks
www.ksbrooks.com

13. Advertise on websites. Try BlogAds.com you might find some cheap advertising spots!
-Jan Fischer-Wade
www.janfischerwade.com

14. Set up Google alerts at www.google.com/alerts to track success and find others talking about your topic, so you can approach them with an article pitch or write on their blog. Be the first to comment on a major news blog. NOTE: THIS IS ALSO A GREAT WAY TO GET REVIEWERS! Sometimes the article author's e-mail or website is there, and you can write them, "I noticed your article about...Perhaps you'd like to review my new book on that topic." Don't hesitate to spend money by mailing out books for review—this is the cheapest advertising you will ever find!
-Susan Schenck, Lac
www.livefoodfactor.com

15. Nothing sells a book better than an author. My number one tip, as the author of the new book *California Girl Chronicles,* is to line up a book tour of genre-specific literary festivals and fairs and do direct outreach with readers. Make sure you have bookmarks made to give away to at least brand your book with those who don't buy it on the spot. A book tour right to the readers gives authors a chance to talk to their audience, sign books (readers love signed copies), and find out reactions to the cover and how to best sell the book. You will sell way more books through direct outreach with your audience than by simple reviews or advertisements.
-Michelle Gamble-Risley
www.3lpublishing.com

16. Encourage readers to take photographs of themselves with your book and to e-mail the pictures to you or share them on Facebook and other social sites. Then share the pictures on your website, blog, Facebook page, Google Plus account, and/or Twitter account. Link to the submitters' sites or mention their social media handles. It gives them some visibility and recognition, and you get a fabulous collection of reader-submitted photos of your book that look cool on your website and social media pages and engage your fans. Inevitably, someone will send in a funny picture (e.g., a cat reading your book). Funny pictures increase the odds that others will share the image, too—further spreading the word about your book.

-Anita Campbell
www.visualmarketingbook.com

17. **The best thing I did was committing a portion of all proceeds to charity,** but I was not specific to which one. This way, I have been able to partner with different organizations to raise money for them, while they raised my profile for me—a win-win!

-Stephanie Staples
www.YourLifeUnlimited.ca

18. **Participate in Goodreads! Notice I said participate, not just join.** Goodreads is an interactive and reciprocal tool for building real relationships with readers—readers who like to share their thoughts in reviews. Just look at how many reviews of a single title, say *Tempest Rising* by Nicole Peeler, there are on Goodreads. Now check to see how many there are on Amazon. Surprising, isn't it? Many of my new readers tell me they bought my book based on what certain reviewers said because they have come to trust those reviewers' opinions. How can you get to know these readers/reviewers better? Be a participant first, a bookseller last, and follow these simple steps:
follow readers' reviews join and participate in communities list books you've read and are reading have an RSS feed of your blog on your author page thank readers if they add your book to their TBR pile

-Heidi Ruby Miller
www.heidirubymiller.blogspot.com

19. **Look for inexpensive ways to advertise in print.** For example, I write about eating and weight; and for $25, I took out an ad in a booklet that was going to the audience of a show about eating disorders that was running for several nights.
Sign up for HARO and ReporterConnection, and seek out interviews on your topic or ones looking for authors. One simple way to promote yourself is simply to say you're an author when you meet people. I'm a psychotherapist and an author, and I often lead with the latter rather than the former. After all, the natural question for an author is, "What did you write?" Answer that, and you're often and running.

-Karen R. Koenig, LCSW, M.Ed.
www.eatingnormal.com

20. **Many authors make a big splash in the first few weeks after their book comes out**, then taper off. To be successful, keep up the glam. Marketing takes dedication. Customers may need to see information about your book multiple times before they will buy. So, don't stop after a month. Keep releasing new marketing tactics, even after the "honeymoon." Give them steady teasers and hints until they are so intrigued they must buy the book. Mix it up. After a few months, assess what is working and what isn't. Prune out poor tactics, and put more effort into tactics that are generating sales. Remember that selling books is a business. Approach your efforts with a business mind-set, determination, and flair.*-Candice M. Hughes, PhD* www.candicehughes.com
Authors take these tips and use them! Active promotion is key to selling books, and now you have

options to promote your book in all kinds of ways. Create some buzz, and sell your books. Here's to your success!

MARCIA PETERSON is a columnist for *WOW! Women on Writing* and the editor of WOW!' blog, *The Muffin*. She lives in Northern California with her husband and two children.

Literary Liaisons:
Who's Reading Romance Books?

ENTERTAINMENT

Summer is the season of beach reads, which means millions of Americans are sitting in the sun with a romance book (or e-book) in hand.

Who's reading these steamy stories? The fan base is a broader group than you might think, as recent popular titles have welcomed new readers to the genre in the past few years. According to Nielsen's Romance Book Buyer Report, romance book buyers are getting younger—with an average age of 42, down from 44 in 2013. This makes the genre's average age similar to the age for fiction overall. In addition, 44% of these readers are aged 18-44, which includes the coveted Millennial demographic.

<u>Romance book buyers are still more likely to be female than buyers of fiction overall,</u> but with more attention than ever directed to the genre—especially given all the media coverage of *Fifty Shades of Grey*—more men are coming into the fold. In first-quarter 2014, men accounted for 15% of romance books purchased, compared with 12% in 2013.

These demographic changes aside, the general profile of romance fans in the U.S. remains fairly steady. Nielsen data shows that romance book buyers are more likely to be from the South and Mid-West regions, tend to be retired and identify as Christian.

These core romance fans are avid readers who stay very loyal to the genre. Some 6% of buyers purchase romance books more than once a week, and 15% do so at least once a week. Moreover, 25% of buyers read romance more than once a week, and nearly half do so at least once a week; only 20% read romance less than once a month.

Younger buyers (those under 30) are not quite as devoted, reading and purchasing less often. They also have different tastes; while romantic suspense is the most popular subgenre overall, these younger readers trend more toward erotic stories.

How are romance readers discovering and purchasing these novels? Both the bookstore and online sources are equally important in the romance market, with Amazon (and Kindle apps for e-books) dominating the online space.

Bookstores remain an important channel for many. Among readers of all ages, buying in the store is the most-mentioned (56%) way of acquiring romance books. Brick-and-mortar stores are also important to discovery. When asked to pick from list of 25 methods of finding romance books, the largest share of fans (66%) chose browsing in a store; also important are in-person recommendations from friends and others they know (54%), online book sites (42%) and bestseller lists (33%).

While bookstores cannot be ignored as a place where many romance fans discover and purchase their next read, the genre is also at the forefront of the digital revolution. The e-book share of romance (39% in Q1 2014) has consistently been above that of adult fiction (31% in Q1 2014) as a whole.

Amazon is the top digital retailer for romance, with 60% of romance e-book readers saying they buy titles via Amazon. When it comes to digital devices, most romance e-book purchasers (83%) say they read via a mobile app on a tablet rather than a dedicated e-reader (12%), with 5% using other devices. Again, Amazon dominates, with the company's Kindle app used by 61% of romance e-book readers.

The lower cost and easy accessibility associated with e-books makes this audience especially open to trying new things. Of those readers who buy digital romance novels, around half agree to a "high extent" that they are more "willing to experiment because the price is low" and "e-books are a good way to try a new author."

So how is the romance audience deciding on which new authors to try? Recommendations from family/friends, reviews, price, teaser chapters and word-of-mouth are the leading influencers cited by readers (each by around 40% of buyers). With over one-third of digital romance readers using subscription providers, e-book recommendation services such as BookBub are also increasingly important for discovery. But age matters in terms of influence; younger romance readers are more likely to be influenced by Amazon ratings and book bloggers, compared to their older counterparts.

Marketing Self-Published Fine Art Photography Books

Meredith Kaminek self-published a book of her fine art photography, together with her own inspirational writings, and then set about publicizing, marketing, and selling her books without the aid of a publisher or publicist. Here's how...

By creating her own opportunities for art shows and book signings, and by making herself easily accessible to anyone interested in her work, she has turned what many fine art photographers might see as a Herculean task into a success.

To date, she has sold almost 2,000 copies and continues to be successful.

Here's how she did it...

From her studio to a creek in the woods, Meredith Kaminek has cultivated her career as a professional portrait photographer since 1992. Connecting with people and who they are, more than what they look like, has always been the true passion in her artistic eye.

With a great connection to nature, Meredith has branched out to share her perspective of how everyday life and our natural surroundings are genuine gifts, as long as we take the time to look at it that way.

Meredith's recently published hard cover book, which is a collection of her photographs of nature – untouched, coupled with simple thoughts and inspirations.

Here are some of the great topics we talked about during our chat in this episode:

- How Meredith first became interested in photography...

- Ways that Meredith markets her portrait and fine art photography…

- The inspiration behind creating a book of fine art photography…

- The exact steps Meredith took to create the book…

- Self-publishing explained…

- Getting out there to promote and sell the book…

- The role of social media in Meredith's online marketing…

- Why the typical fine art photography sales website doesn't work as expected…

- The most common mistakes new fine art photographers make…

- How photographers can simply get out of their own way…

Book Cover Success and Failure Explained

BY JOEL FRIEDLANDER ON JUNE 9, 2014 # 33 COMMENTS

Not that long ago I was asked to create a presentation that would help authors when it came time to design a book cover. I know that there are lots of do-it-yourselfers who are self-publishers, and there are also authors who are buying services from professionals. I wanted to create a presentation that would give both kinds of authors useful information.

Since I've been judging book covers for a long time (and hundreds more in the monthly Ebook Cover Design Awards) I know how difficult it can be for an author to see her book cover objectively. Especially for first-time authors, it can be a real and difficult challenge to step back and try to see your book cover as a selling vehicle for your book, and not as an extension of your own identity.

Your Book Cover Has a Job to Do

Let's face it, there are hundreds of different genres, different kinds of books, and different ways to solve the problem presented by the need to create a cover-a brand, an image, an exemplar, an avatar-for your book. Taking that vast variety into account, and confining myself to books that their authors hope to sell commercially, it seemed like there were 5 separate tasks your book cover has to accomplish:

Announce its genre

Clearly, many book buyers search for books by category, niche, or genre, so this instant identification with where your book belongs is a critical task.

Telegraph its tone

Although more subtle, it's also important to imply the tone of a work, especially fiction. Is it a brash, over-the-top page turner, or a subtle character study?

Explain its scope

More common to nonfiction, readers need to know what's included in your book and what's not-in terms of subject matter, time periods, geography, skill levels, or any other guide that will give potential buyers this information.

Generate excitement

Effective book covers have a "hook"-something that intrigues, grabs you by the throat, makes a promise-something that will attract and hold a reader's attention and make them want to know more.

Establish a market position

Your book cover can help browsers by letting them know where your book fits in with other, similar books they are already familiar with. More encyclopedic? With vampires? And tons of resources?

Book Covers Often Fail These Tasks

Looking at the books that did not meet these criteria, I was able to identify some main reasons for their failure:

They are illegible.

Although it seems that the least we can expect of a book cover is to be able to read it-both the type and any images used-many covers were either unreadable or just plain hard to make out.

They disregard their genre or niche

Maybe you're publishing a thriller, and want to attract readers who enjoy thrillers. If you put a cover on your book that makes it look more like a history or an academic paper, won't it be harder to interest those readers? Many book covers fail this test.

There's no "hook"

Maybe that "sunset on the ocean" was incredibly meaningful for the author, or connected to a crucial scene in the story, but we don't know that, do we? These books present no particular reason to even pick up the book to find out more. In a word, they are boring.

They are graphically or typographically incompetent

This is the biggest challenge for novice book cover designers. It's not that easy to learn typography, or how to composite images in an image editing program. Too many books show the results: incomprehensible images, inappropriate fonts, and tortured special effects, all filling the vacuum left by the absence of any real design.

Some Concepts to Analyze and Cure Book Cover Failures

You can solve these problems, and in reviewing my work to this point, I realized that the answers usually came from just 3 places.

Focus-Successful book covers have a specific point of view and are dedicated to communicating a very clear message.

This takes focus and knowing what's of interest to your readers. It can also mean using design skills to control the readers "eyepath" as they look at the cover, so you are focusing them on the information you want to communicate.

Contrast-Book covers without contrast can be monotone in color, weak in the fonts chosen and how they are used, or have very busy backgrounds that distract attention from the main communication. Using contrast wisely with colors, fonts, and combined elements will clarify your message.

Positioning-Your need to indicate the genre and tone of your book, while also letting readers know what they can expect from the book, come together to help place your book in context with other books. Establishing this position makes your book understandable to more of your readers and lets them know what your book is all about.

There's More to a Great Cover

This analysis of what makes book covers succeed or fail is a way to look at covers you're creating, or designs someone else is proposing to you. But of course, a lot more goes into a great cover. No matter what category, niche, or genre your book is, you'll also need:

A great title (and subtitle), especially for nonfiction books where keywords will help draw prospects. To make sure your cover fits your printer's specifications. More on that below. Back cover copy that's finely crafted marketing copy.

Targeted testimonials, ones that will be meaningful to your readers, and which will help convince people to buy.   °

Your book available in as many formats as possible, depending on the individual book.

Technical Book Cover Construction

The one place DIY authors seem to need help, especially if they don't know professional layout software like Adobe InDesign, is with properly laying out their cover. In order to do this, you'll need to account for things like: changing your spine width depending on your printer, paper, and page count, establishing "safe zones" of .25 inches to keep critical type and images away from the trim and fold edges, creating .25 "bleed" areas extending off the edges of the cover while maintaining the proper final trim size.

At least with these technical requirements, help is a little easier to come by, and later I'll tell you exactly what I mean. If you've tried creating your own book covers-especially in Microsoft Word-what obstacles did you encounter? There are eight cover design secrets publishers use to manipulate readers into buying books. Indie publishers are slowly coming to realize the importance of an amazing book cover. Since many self-publishing authors are starting out on a very small budget however, book covers are still a popular choice. But be forewarned: although book cover designs come in a wide variety, publishers consistently use reliable, time-tested techniques and guidelines to catch your attention and make the sale.

You want your cover to be different and unique, but you also want to tick all the right boxes. The worst thing an author can do is consider their cover design like a blank canvas and add whatever they want, wherever they want. So here are the tricks you need to know. (Note: I chose these images and book covers quickly to illustrate my point).

Make it "Pop"

A lot of authors ask for covers that "pop." And many designers have no idea what this means. But I've narrowed it down to contrast. You want a strong light to dark transition, with strong shadows. You want the central object or character to really "pop" out, by being spotlighted and lighter in color (you can also do the reverse and have a very light cover, with a bold, dark central image). But you also want contrasting colors: colors that are opposites on a color wheel. Movie posts use orange and teal all the time, because they are a very pleasing color combination. You can also use blue and red (although it's hard to do well - black/gray and red usually works better), purple and yellow (colors which - I believe, only those born in Aquarius truly love). (Note: non-fiction covers don't need to "pop" in the same way - they can stand out by using bright colors or a simple central image).

Lots of space

A lot of book covers are too busy. Many of mine certainly are (partly due to my design style, partly because the authors want to include everything on the cover). Even if there are lots of elements, the background should be blended together smoothly - this can be done with a color wash (for example, in Fallen, the dress could have "popped" more if it were deep red… but that would have made the text harder to read.

Some covers are breathtaking, but very simple. Here's a quick rule of thumb: non-fiction appeals to the brain. You want an instantly clever image to catch their mental attention. Non-fiction covers should have a central "gimmick" and a solid color background or gradient (orange and yellow are very popular for business books. So fiction covers should be bursting with color, vibrancy, action. They should be beautiful. The art alone should make you feel, something like longing or loss or passion, immediately.

Be careful of over using drop shadows through, I try to avoid them by using natural contrast (put light text on dark areas of the cover). So when designing for fiction, you're appealing to the subconscious and the emotions. You're not providing detail for the brain. Focus on colors, abstract symbols, representations. Focus on strong contrast and mood and how does the cover make you feel.

Tips for Marketing Self-Published Children's Books

Marketing self-published children's books requires appealing to both kids and adults

By Alex Palmer |

Social media and other online tools have made it easier than ever for authors to connect with readers, but they've also made it more difficult for self-published titles to stand out. Authors of self-published children's books, in particular, have their marketing work cut out for them. Promotions for these titles have to appeal to two distinct groups: kids and the adults, such as parents and grandparents, who might buy books for them.

Fancy Miss Pig

by
Doris Pyrant White
Illustrated by Hunter Murray

"You must market to both the child who will be at the library picking out his or her book and the adult who will ultimately be the one to buy the book for the child," says Tiffany Papageorge, who self-published the children's book *My Yellow Balloon*. "Marketing an adult book is not nearly as complicated."

Papageorge's efforts to connect with these buyers have included an active social media presence and outreach to "mommy blogs," as well as live events at schools and bookstores. This combination of marketing efforts and steady sales attracted the interest of the independent publisher Sourcebooks, which reached out to her about setting up a traditional publishing deal and distributing the book. But after reviewing the costs and benefits of a more traditional route, Papageorge opted to continue her indie approach.

Authors can engage parents and groups on social media using the topics in their books to start or join relevant conversations. If parents are discussing ways to deal with bullying or making friends at a new school, an author whose book addresses these topics can chime in.

Full-color print editions are the norm for children's books, which can mean a significant cost for each book ordered via print-on-demand. An author can arrange for distribution through a company like Baker & Taylor, which will also allow books to be advertised in its catalogs. And services like Lulu and Amazon's CreateSpace allow for authors to print and sell books as they are ordered.

Fan Involvement

A book often gets its most important endorsements from fans, and that is especially true of children's books: enthusiastic parents and their kids become near evangelists for the characters they love. Tapping these resources can begin in the book's planning stages, by spreading the word through a Kickstarter or Indiegogo campaign, for example. This helps increase awareness of an author's project while raising money for production and distribution, and testing whether there is strong enough interest to proceed. Services like Inkshares combine the crowdfunding approach with publishing services, providing design, printing, and distribution (and 50% royalties) to books that meet their preorder goals.

Authors can also find more personal ways to connect fans with their books. Alonda Williams wrote *Penny and the Magic Puffballs*, in part, to help give her African-American daughter confidence about wearing her hair differently from other girls in her class. Williams connected with potential fans online by creating a Facebook page for the character and holding a contest for parents to take a photo of their daughters wearing their hair in "puffballs." Williams then included some of these photos in the back of the book, getting more interest from followers. She then gave away a free copy of the book each day for the 15 days leading up to its launch.

"I was able to get over 1,000 fans in the first three days and have leveled off at around 11,000 fans," Williams says. The book has since sold more than 5,000 copies and she has a follow-up coming out in a few weeks.

Create Memorable Events

Events can be a major opportunity for children's book authors, but a straightforward reading usually won't be enough to keep kids' attention and open their parents' pocketbooks. "We have authors that write in other genres as well, but we find that children's books can be the most effective for self-pubbed authors to get events," says Julie Schoerke, founder of JKS Communications, a literary publicity firm that worked with traditionally published authors for years before adding self-published authors to its stable.

Children's books lend themselves to high-energy interactions with young readers. Authors looking to make events part of their marketing plans might want to consider ways to add extra fun and games. For example, Sharyn Shields recently held an event for her book *The Wisdom of Dr. Soles*, about a plain shoe who learns to accept herself for what she is.

Shields created life-size models of the shoe characters from her book—with names like Plain Jane, Miss Diva, and Road Runner—and performed selections at a farmers' market at the mixed-use Serenbe urban community outside of Atlanta. "The models were very successful in drawing children to my table at the Serenbe Farmers Market from a distance so that I could interact with them further and get them involved with the book," Shields says. "Reporters were also interested in the 3-D visual display. I've been contacted for an interview for a local magazine by the editor who was impressed with the crowd response to the life-sized models from the book."

Distribution Challenges

Indie authors continue to face difficulties when it comes to getting access to schools and libraries. "It's virtually impossible to get statewide library awards that launch an author onto summer or school reading lists like traditionally published books," Schoerke says.

With so many writers already struggling to get their titles noticed, indie authors need to put extra effort into getting schools interested in hosting their events. Kristy Short—whose Zanda Humphrey series includes *Operation Nice*, about a fourth grader who creates a robot to fight bullying—got creative in marketing her book to schools and parents for educational events.

"What finally got me into schools was developing a one-hour antibullying assembly/workshop around [*Operation Nice*]," Short says. "The story resonated with the kids and the assembly was a success." Over the years, she has spoken before some 5,000 kids and "sold a lot of books" in the process.

Kevin Christofora took a similar approach in marketing *The Hometown All Stars*, which offers instructions on the basics of Little League baseball and aims to both entertain kids and offer guidance to coaches. This means a built-in audience, and Christofora reached out to regional and state Little League groups, not just to advertise the book but to suggest ways that it could be incorporated into the organizations' fund-raising efforts.

Kevin Christofora marketed his Hometown All Stars series to youth sports leagues.

"I offered the book at cost, so the groups could add $5 to the registration fee so every kid gets a free book," Christofora says. "It helps to start driving education before they start their first day and makes it easy for parents."

Shields has also found success in partnering with organizations on events and gatherings for *The Wisdom of Dr. Soles*. She offers presentations at schools, asking teachers or administrators to recommend students to help play characters or narrate the story in front of other students, making the experience more engaging for everyone. "I've also had event bookings with youth organizations like the Girl Scouts and Diamond in the Rough," Shields says. "The Wisdom of Dr. Soles gives me a fun way to teach young children that everyone has their own unique talents and inherent value."

Papageorge urges authors to get as much face time with the leaders of such organizations as possible. "Most organizations have their own conferences. Find out where they are and get a booth," she says. "As much as social media can bring about mass awareness, there truly isn't anything as impactful or meaningful as human-to-human contact, because presence fosters an authentic experience for both sides."

Expand the Network

Of course, authors don't have to host actual live events to achieve marketing success. There is an extensive community of children's book writers worth tapping. For example, the Society of Children's Book Writers and Illustrators boasts more than 22,000 members and 70 regional chapters, hosting conferences throughout the year at which writers, illustrators, editors, publishers, and agents can meet and interact.

Authors should also never underestimate the power of their own friends and families. "My theory was to follow the money," says Mary Stern, who self-published her Cowboy Dog series, about a boy, his grandmother, and the eponymous canine. "I called former CEOs and executives that I worked with during my corporate days. They bought hundreds of books. Many gave books to their employees; others donated books to children's hospitals."

Laura Barta made her *My China Travel Journal* part of a full set of interactive educational toys.

Williams has found targeted Facebook ads to be a crucial ingredient in building a following and generating interest in *Penny and the Magic Puffballs*. "The key to success intimately knows your audience before you start marketing," she says. "Social media, especially advanced analytics on Facebook, allows you to target your audience very effectively. Facebook, Twitter, and Instagram have all been very helpful. However, Facebook offers the best campaign targeting."

Children's titles also lend themselves to merchandise and giveaways—and authors should consider offering bookmarks, posters, or other items featuring the book's characters as sales incentives. Laura Barta took this approach even further with her 2011 self-published book, *My China Travel Journal*, which follows a pair of American children as they visit China and learn about its culture and cuisine. Barta founded Whole World Wide Toys, a toy company, to include the book as a learning tool in its World Village Playset China. The set also includes color story cards for reading comprehension, a fabric play mat, and standup puzzle pieces.

"I created World Village Playsets to add an element of creative play to the reading experience. The play mat features several artistic details that are culturally accurate and featured prominently in the story line to help children become more familiar with China," Barta says. "I believe that kids can learn in many different ways, and they can have fun while they learn."

A version of this article appeared in the 07/27/2015 issue of *Publishers Weekly* under the headline: Not Child's Play

Three Approaches to Publishing Your Photo Book

ALLEN MURABAYASHI

There comes a point in a photographer's life when publishing a book seems like a logical step. The coffee table book represents a platonic ideal for a photo project that is both long-term and worthy of considerations by others. Yet, even with the advent of high quality on-demand solutions like Blurb, book publishing is still fraught with challenges. Here are three different approaches to book publishing in the 21st century.

Traditional: Larger publishing houses with a pedigreed history and established distribution channels.

Independent Publishing (aka Small Press Publishing): Typically a publisher with less revenue per year than a large established publishing house and less than 10-15 books published per year.

Self-publishing (e-publishing and print on demand): The photographer and writer are responsible for all aspects of production, marketing and sales.

Motivation

Before embarking on a book project of any size, understand your motivation for doing so. Most book projects fail to sell even 1,000 copies, and thus can drain considerable resources without much return on investment.

Vanity projects are likely to lose money, so it's important to identify whether an audience exists for your book, and if so, who they are. Publishing the content through traditional or social media can be indicative of interest, and publishers can often provide valuable opinions on the viability of any book idea.

Considering Costs

There are two primary categories of costs to consider: soft costs, and cost of goods sold.

Soft costs: Fees associated with design, editing, copywriting, proofreading.

You can take a completely DIY (do-it-yourself) approach to producing a book, but many photographers outsource specific tasks to experts. Soft costs can range from $0 to the low tens of thousands of dollars.

COGS: "costs of goods sold," or your unit price to produce a book.
COGS can vary wildly depending on the size, number of pages, and materials used in your book. General edition photo books fall into a range of pricing with a sweet spot from $30 to $60.

To drive a profit, you need to control your COGS, and something like a heavier stock paper or large dimensions could easily throw you into the red. You need to familiarize yourself with the various materials options and their related costs before embarking on any book project.

Three Approaches to Photo Book Publishing

#1: Traditional Publishing
After 40 years of photographing some of the most iconic nature and wildlife photos, Thomas Mangelsen decided to throw together a retrospective entitled "The Last Great Wild Places." As a well-established photographer and author with multiple titles under his belt, Mangelsen was approached by esteemed publisher Rizzoli, which had previously published or distributed three other titles for him.

But even with interest from a publisher, Mangelsen warns of a contracting market, "According to my colleagues and the word on the street including most large publishers, photographic coffee table books are unfortunately a shrinking market. They are still being published but not in the numbers they were 20 or even 10 years ago."

A distinguishing factor that makes the proposition of a large format coffee table book more economically viable for Mangelsen is his ownership of eight galleries around the country combined with a large following both online and in real life. With "The Last Great Wild Places, Mangelsen created three editions to address a wide audience, including a limited special edition book aimed at hard core collectors of his work.

Unlike independent or self-publishing, working with a publisher meant more delegation of duties. Mangelsen said, "[My team] worked with the publisher on the format and size and approximate number of pages. We collected content and then edited from hundreds of thousands of possible images down to roughly 300 that we then sent to Rizzoli to be laid out by their designer…We went through several design concepts and drafts. We considered use of full bleeds, double page spreads, number of images on a spread, white space, authors for written text and forward, number of words, paper samples and varnishes to determine which materials would best represent my vision for the book. Once we had the book fully proofed my publisher handled most of the interactions with the printer who they had recommended."

As far as costs, Rizzoli was responsible for the layout, design, purchasing materials and printing and the author. Mangelsen covered the cost of his office staff working on the book's content, as well as purchasing from the publisher to sell through his galleries and website.

The traditional publisher brings two major advantages to the table: distribution and marketing. This includes negotiating shelf space and promotion at bookstores as well as coordinating special sales through book clubs and online retailers like Amazon. Generating PR, mailing out advance copies to book reviewers, etc can be done by independent publishers, but large publishers have staff, know-how and connections that help to increase the visibility of the titles they represent.

Still, publishing a book is challenging even for seasoned authors, and this book was no different for Mangelsen. "All books have their own challenges. From getting the content, to editing, layout and design, printing and binding, collaborating with publishers and writers and distribution and sales, books are a labor of love…There will be road bumps, such as the binding issues that delayed the release of my latest book, but fortunately working with Rizzoli they resolved the issues in time to have a great product for the holiday season. "

Despite a movement to digital publishing and online content consumption, Mangelsen finds himself in a unique place. "Since I have somewhat of a special niche, having my own galleries, website and other social media I find that most of my customers and limited edition print collectors want to have a physical book that they can look at as opposed to a digital version. Because my built-in audiences I have been able to continue creating books and been successful in making large format coffee table books."

Pros:
– Many aspects of design & production delegated to publisher
– Distribution and marketing also handled by publisher
Cons:
– Might not receive a % of sales after author fee

#2: Independent Publishing

As the 20th anniversary of <u>Scott Strazzante</u>'s personal project documenting the Harlow Cagwin farm in Illinois, Scott Strazzante started thinking about the best way to memorialize the effort. Strazzante had been showing the project through speaking engagements, multiple publications and a MediaStorm video, and during that time, many people inquired about the book version.

"I, literally, had hundreds of people ask me when the book was coming out, so, I was confident that there would be a market for *Common Ground*. However, I, also, knew for the book to be truly successful, I would have to sell to non-photographers, also."

Strazzante intended to self-publish the book and had a preliminary book design by <u>Deb Pang Davis</u>when he created <u>a Kickstarter campaign</u>. But beyond the intent and design, he didn't really know much else. "I was naive about the world of book publishing when I started the Kickstarter campaign. I really had no idea what self-publishing meant or how much work was involved in producing a book. In hindsight, I should have done a lot more legwork before securing the funds."

The success of the Kickstarter project provided Strazzante with a way to gauge the appetite for the content while raising $46k and bringing new eyeballs to the project. But crowdfunding isn't without its challenges. "My big mistake was underestimating the amount of time it would take to get the book finished." Strazzante's initial estimate of November 2013, stretched another year before the book made into the hands of the backers.

Also, getting physical addresses. "Kickstarter doesn't require people to give their addresses when they pledge support, so that all has to be done after the fact…At this point, I still don't have addresses for about 75 of the donors." Strazzante also notes that the personal project was difficult to balance. "Also, with a full-time job, it has

been a struggle to get all the rewards out in a timely manner. I still have a handful of prints to send out."

Strazzante was contacted by a publisher, but after some negative internal reviews he cut ties. "The two anonymous reviewers didn't like the book. One wrote that some of the diptychs were redundant (which I agree with) while the other said that it was obvious that all the suburban photos were fake and that the photographer had shown the farm photos to the residents and had them recreate them."

Strazzante then reached out to Warren Winter at PSG Wire, an independent publisher. Strazzante's strong social media presence was attractive to Winter, but the photos and story were equally as compelling. "The story Scott tells in *Common Ground* is one that I felt would resonate far beyond the photo community. It has such a strong universal message to remind us that we are all far more alike than we are different." Winter normally engages a project much earlier in the lifecycle, providing image editing and design guidance. But in this case, Scott went back and re-edited the material with Mike Davis, redesigned the book with Deb Pang Davis, obtained a foreword by David Guttenfelder, and hired Editor Lynne Warren to write captions for the image.

Winter worked with Strazzante on proofing, printing and marketing. Generally speaking, the publisher will decide (or help the photographer decide) on aspects of production like hard or paperback, paper stock, coating, binding options, jacket options, cloth options, printing options (stochastic vs half-tone), shrink wrapping, freight, insurance, customs, trucking, warehousing, order fulfillment, etc.

Book size (both the physical dimensions and number of pages) can dramatically swing the cost of producing a book. But Winter provided the following ballpark estimate for:

– 8.5" x 11" hardcover
– Heavier stock with no special varnish
– 192 pages
– Dust jacket or cloth cover
– 1000 copies
– Approximately $14,000

This price does not include the cost of a designer ($30-100/page), editor ($500-$5000/project), proofreader, writer, or any other consultants.

Winter believes independent publishers act as gatekeepers. "The toughest thing to do is tell someone who has spent years creating a great story that you don't think it's marketable in book form." He vehemently opposes "vanity" publishers who don't invest their own money and resources into the project. "I see too many indie publishers take on any project where the photographer raised all the money on their own so they, the publisher, have no real skin in the game, and they don't pull their full back into marketing and publicity."

Strazzante believes that the photographer must keep the project and book on people's minds through social media and more. He's relied upon the relationships and good will that he's built up over his career. "I have made a lot of friends over the years in the business and many are now in places of power. The ones that I have reached out to have been very kind in promoting the project or spreading the word amongst their friends and colleagues."

Can a photographer profit in independent publishing? In short, yes, but it's rare. Winter believes that photographers have to be very objective before embarking on a book project. "[Photographers] have to be honest with themselves on whether or not the story will appeal only to other photographers or if it will have broader mass market appeal."

He points out the success of another PSG book, "That Tree" by Mark Hirsh, which has sold over 8,000 copies. "75% of those have been sold directly through our site, so we keep 100% of the cover price. I think too many indie publishers rely too heavily on retail sales...retailers take anywhere from 40% to 55% of the cover price." Winter breaks down the economics for 1,000 copies of a book.
– Printing, proofing, binding and ocean freight: $14,000
– Design: $5,000

– General Marketing: $2,000
– Total: $21,000, or $21 per unit.

If you sell 500 books at $50 through Barnes and Noble at a 55% discount, you net $22.50/book. After COGS (costs of goods sold), your total net = $750.
If you sell 250 books at $50 through Amazon.com, you net $40/book. After COGS, our total net = $4,750.
If you sell the remaining 250 books directly at $50, you net $29/book. After COGS, your total net = $7,250.
Total net revenue for 1,000 books sold = $12,750.

But 95% of all photo books never sell more than 1,000 copies. Winter warns, "You can clearly see how a high COGS will make selling in retail virtually nothing more than a break even proposition."

Despite all the challenges, Strazzante is thrilled with the results. "When this is all over, I will come out in the black on the Kickstarter campaign and, if the books sell, I will make additional money on the extra books that the Kickstarter money allowed me to have printed. It has been a lot more work than I ever imagined, but it was totally worthwhile."

Pros:
– Good option for niche titles
– Photographer can exert more control over project
Cons:
– Distribution channels more limited
– No big name marketing machine

#3: E-Publishing and Print on Demand

Dave Black has had a long and storied career, and his images have been featured in over 50 book projects. But he had never had a book of his own, despite having been approached by multiple publishers in the past.

His motivation for pursuing a book project came down to his daughter. "[It] began as a personal project in which I could tell my career story to my daughter, how I got started, why I make the pictures I do, and how she could make pictures too."

When he initiated the project, Black was unconcerned with the market for the book. "Selling it to the public was not primary and only came as an afterthought once I got involved in the writing and design, but offering it in the marketplace did not affect how I designed it or what I wrote. I made it just the way I wanted."

He quickly decided that self-publishing was the most economically feasible route. "If I were to have gone through a publisher like Simon and Schuster the book would have cost me $30,000 up front…That would mean I would need to sell 8,571 books (at an average price of $50.95) just to break even financially."

After consulting with some colleagues, Black decided to print on demand with Blurb.com based on product quality, price, layout flexibility, and the variety of book sizes. A three month process of designing and proofing all the material himself led to a gorgeous 120 page book that costs him $88.95 to print, and which he sells for $98.95. The goal of making money was secondary to producing a quality book that was both entertaining and educational. Since the book's debut in April 2009, the sales of hardcopies have slowed down to approximately 5 per month. Black did release a digital version in 2009, but it was only available as an app through the Apple App Store at a price of $5, which was split 50/50 with Apple. So in 2011, he removed the App version, and relied solely on a PDF-based computer edition. "I released the current Digital edition in September 2014." For $29.95, customers can purchase and download a PDF version of the book for tablets and computers. It's three times the profit with no physical inventory, nor fulfilment logistics. The only fees he pays are for the PayPal transaction.

Black only markets the book through his website and at his lectures. This low-key approach is in keeping with his personality, and it suits him just fine. He has a ready-made, targeted audience through this approach.

Producing the book took about two months from start to finish with Black working on the project for a few hours about three days a week. The endeavor has been profitable, but Black is quick to remind that the project was motivated by passion rather than money. "I'm a hero in my own house, what could be more rewarding. Have they been profitable…yes, but that wasn't the goal. Thousands of people, most likely photographers have purchased [my two] books in all their editions. I receive emails from many who have learned something valuable about photography and thus improved their photographic skills because of reading them. That is also very rewarding to me." The process has been so rewarding, that Black is working on his third book entitled "Lightpainting."

Pros:
– Very low overhead costs
– You can literally DIY
– No middlemen
– High profit margin for electronic version
Cons:
– High COGS for printed book
– Lower profit margins
– Constrained by materials offered by printing service

About the author: Allen Murabayashi is the Chairman and co-founder of PhotoShelter, which regularly publishes resources for photographers. Allen is a graduate of Yale University.

How to Get a Self-Published Book Into Bookstores

If you're one of many authors who have self-published a book and you want to get that book into bookstores, have a plan and persevere. While it may not turn into a bestseller, you will have the satisfaction of readership and local representation for your work.

1. **Start <u>promoting your book</u> before contacting bookstores to show that you're serious, then continue promoting it and directing potential customers to the stores that are willing to stock your book.**

<u>Create a website</u> or blog for the book.

<u>Create a press kit.</u> Describe the book and provide contact information. Include only the most influential or glowing reviews. Leave out irrelevant information such as your personal resume. You have about 60 seconds to make an impression with it, so make sure your strongest selling points are on the first page.

<u>Send press releases to local newspapers and bookstores.</u> It will be much more effective if you send these to individual contact people, so make some phone calls or do some research to find out the specific person who reviews books in each company.

<u>Advertise in local publications</u>. Let your bookstore contact person know that you're marketing the book locally. Offer to put an "available at ..." line in future ads if they will accept the book for sale.

- <u>Contact local TV and radio stations for interviews.</u> Again, having the name of a contact person will make your efforts more productive. If you have mutual friends, ask them to recommend you to media people they know.

- <u>Offer to hold author readings at libraries</u> and writing conferences to increase your visibility.

- Create fliers containing information about your book. Include the ISBN and a brief synopsis. Leave the flyers on public bulletin boards to create local interest.
- Enlist your network. Ask your friends, neighbors, family, and co-workers-to request the book at their local bookstores. Then resist the temptation to sell your book to those people yourself. Ask them to wait to buy it from the store so that there is a history of good sales.

2. **Ask the store to order your book from their distributors.** If your book is available through national distributors such as Ingram or Baker & Taylor, the bookstore can order directly from the distributor and may be willing to do so just from a phone call. Taking books one-at-a-time on consignment from the author, on the other hand, is much more time-consuming (and thus less profitable) for bookstores than going through an established distributor, which automates reordering, returns, and payments.

3. **If they aren't interested in stocking physical copies - or even if they are, in ADDITION to the print copies - ask about opportunities to promote the eBook version.** Through a partnership between the American Booksellers Association (local independent bookstores) and Kobo Inc, bookstores can sell eBooks and earn a percentage of all device and eBook sales.

4. **Identify the bookstore contact person.** If you are distributing your book yourself, call the bookstore and ask who handles their "consignment" or "local author" books. Start with chain bookstores to get experience with the process; then approach independent bookstores, which are more likely to have a Local Authors section. If you are a local author, the bookstore will be more likely to accept your book as a community service than if you're some distant author who will not be doing local promotion. Ask if you can make an appointment to come in and show them the book.

5. **Be professional and respectful.** At your meeting with the bookstore contact, distinguish yourself from pushy self-published authors by being easy to work with.

- <u>When contacting the bookstore</u>, saying that your book is available through online-only booksellers or your personal website is not a selling point; compared with reputable publishers, these methods are used heavily for the "vanity" publishing of books that did not have high enough quality for traditional publishing.
- <u>Although you may be a long-time customer of that bookstore</u>, you are now the seller and *they* are the customer. It's fine to say that you love the store (if you do), but don't pressure them to take your book just because you've bought a lot of books from them in the past.
- <u>Be prepared to leave a copy of the book with the manager or buyer</u> for evaluation. Let them know that you would be available for author signings and readings when the time comes (meaning "if the book sells").
- <u>Ask the bookstore contact person if they would like a complimentary</u> copy of the book, but don't ask them to read it; they will read your book if they are interested in it.
- <u>It is naive to suggest</u> that the store should put your book on their Staff Recommendations shelf, or that they display it at the front counter. Marketing decisions are made by the bookstore, and only amateurs ask to be placed on the store's top-selling, most visible locations before there is a history of strong sales.
- <u>Do not presume to tell a bookstore that they will "sell a lot of copies."</u> That is out of your hands. Let your results speak for themselves.

6. **Follow up.** Check back periodically with the stores that have taken the book and ask if they need more copies. (Every 6-8 weeks is sufficient.)
7. **Be as professional at the end as at the beginning.** Don't be grudging when the contract time is up and the store asks you to take back unsold copies. They took a chance, and if the book didn't sell, it is largely because the author didn't promote it or send people in to look at it. If you're cheerful and respectful, the bookstore will be much more likely to accept your future work.
8. **Respect staff time.** If you're in a busy bookstore, get in and out as quickly as you can. Once the store accepts the book, you no longer need to "sell" it by talking about yourself or the book. It's actually counter-productive to monopolize staff time and doesn't work to

get the staff to hand-sell your book. Like every other reader, the bookstore contact person will take a quick look at the book and make their own buying/reading decisions.

9. **Continue marketing.** Once you've gotten your self-published book into bookstores, don't stop working. Push the book as hard as you did before to encourage people to buy it. Your book will be restocked, especially by larger chain bookstores, only if sales are good.

10. **How many books should I leave at a time in one book store?**
Discuss this with the store. What terms have you agreed? Where will the book be placed? Are you covered for damages or theft? How much space will the store allocate to your book? How many books does the store want initially?

11. **Is there a difference between being confident and pushy?**

Yes, so you don't want to go too far into the pushy direction. Don't be afraid to walk into stores and talk to the employees or make your book known, but don't stay past your welcome either, and respect anyone who says no.

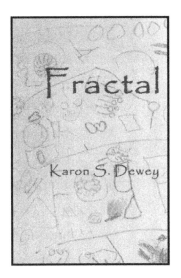

Also research smaller distributors that might work specifically with the type of book you have published, but be aware that a bookstore will not set up an account with an unknown distributor just to have access to your book, so you may need to ask the bookstore to carry it on consignment even if you do have a distributor.

Get an International Standard Book Number (ISBN) and bar code for the book. If you don't have one, the individual bookstore will need to assign one for their in-house use.

Before you publish, contact the major book distributors about carrying your book, which will make it easier for bookstores to take a risk on it. While distributors are paid a portion of the sales, they make it much easier for bookstores to try the book and then return it to the distributor if it doesn't sell.

- Before you publish the book, ask someone from your local bookstore to meet with you to give you guidelines on what kind of books they take on consignment, and what special requirement they may have -- such as a title on the spine of the book.

- Attend publishing trade shows held by national and local booksellers associations. Hand out a business card for the book and your contact information; follow up with a PR packet if they show interest. Trade shows also give you the opportunity to meet buyers, distributors and others working in the publishing and bookselling fields who can offer advice as to how to get a self-published book into bookstores.

- <u>If you're serious about distributing the book yourself,</u> create a marketing plan before you pay for self-publishing, as different self-publishing options have different strengths and limitations.

- <u>Don't take it personally</u> when a store won't stock your book. For a variety of reasons, most of which are out of your control, some stores may not be able to take the book. Be friendly, thank them for their time, and move on.

- <u>Be prepared to take off your</u> "sensitive artist" writer hat and put on your "savvy marketer" distributor hat. It's a different skill set.

Five things your book description says about you

BY BRYAN COHEN

It's tough to write a 70,000 word book, but it's just as tough to write a book description of a few hundred words. Bryan Cohen from Authors outlines some common issues and actionable takeaways to help you improve your book description. Readers learn a lot about you from reading your book description. Unfortunately, the things they glean from your blurb aren't always positive.

The few-hundred-word description of your latest work needs proper time and attention to convey the right messages about you and your books.

Here are five things your description might say about you.

1. You Write Boring Books

Most book descriptions are about as appealing as a moldy sponge. They go to great lengths to name characters (first, last, and middle names), explain side plots, and provide dubiously important information along the way. The final result is that your book sounds boring, and the readers who stumble upon your product description have no reason to question their first impression.

When you take the time to craft an engaging blurb with a strong hook, however, readers get a different impression. If your description effectively conveys the emotion and entertainment of your book, then you can turn casual browsers into buyers.

Takeaway: Use a strong hook and a compelling synopsis to draw readers in.

2. Your Book Is Very Confusing

Somewhere along the way, authors got the strange notion that book descriptions can only have five or six sentences. Instead of questioning this assertion, they've turned their blurbs into a grammar school student's worst sentence diagramming nightmare. Nobody likes a clause junkie who uses four or more commas per sentence. If you're packing your description with overly complex sentence structure, then readers will assume your book is likewise too complicated to understand.

The description is not the time to explain everything there is to know about a character, setting, or plot. You can save the full backstory for the book itself. As you write your blurb, focus on one main character trait and one main plot thread. Too much more will overwhelm the reader and keep her from pressing the buy button. Simple always wins.

Takeaway: Use simpler, declarative sentences and keep backstory and side plots to a minimum.

3. Your Book Isn't Professional

If your description contains grammar or punctuation errors, then readers will assume your book contains errors as well. If your book description is formatted in a strange way or it's one giant blob of text, then readers will guess your book has the same problems. If your book description doesn't seem professional, then readers will assume your book isn't professional.

The easiest fix for this is to get someone else to read your description before you begin your major launch promotions. Don't let a reader or a friend be the one to point out errors in your product description after you've launched. Catch them now to preserve sales later.

Takeaway: Get someone to edit your blurb and double check how it looks online.

4. You Write Books I'm Not Interested In

Let's say you've covered your bases for the above three points. Your description is compelling, concise, and it's free of errors. The next step is to make sure you're effectively conveying the right genre. It isn't enough to put your book in the appropriate category with the proper keywords. If your book is an action-packed thriller but you fail to mention that, then you may lose people who are on the verge of making the purchase.

You may feel silly using flowery adjectives to describe your own book, but you need to think like a publisher. A publishing company would never hold back from trying to sell one of its books. You bet the company would describe an enchanting fantasy novel as "mesmerizing, breathtaking, and a treat for the imagination." You need to do the exact same thing. Don't let your modesty get the best of you.

Takeaway: Make your book sound interesting with appropriate and enticing adjectives.

5. You Don't Care If I Buy Your Book

In an ideal world, our readers would be intently focused on our product description while calmly sipping a mug of tea and marveling at the enormity of their gargantuan checking account balance. In reality, these casual browsers have your book page open on one of 20 Internet tabs while they're keeping the kids from setting the house on fire as they think about the overdue electricity bill. Our potential customers are distracted, they're busy, and they're probably on a budget. To coax them to spend money on your book, you have to encourage them to take action.

Using a clear Call to Action (CTA) at the end of your description is a must. Sometimes just asking a reader to "scroll up and buy to start the adventure today," is enough to cut through the overstimulated, multi-tasking, budget-conscious barriers that block them from purchasing your book. Failure to use a CTA puts you at the mercy of the constant clicking of your overwhelmed potential customer.

Takeaway: Use a Call to Action at the end of your description.

Your work isn't over just because you completed the book. The most important words you write may be part of the simple, emotional, and intriguing description that goes online for all to see. Make sure your blurb sends the right message.

Bryan Cohen

Bryan Cohen is the author of Ted Saves the World, the first book in a YA sci-fi/fantasy series, and a collection of creative writing prompts books. You can find him at www.bryancohen.com.

13 Reasons why Serials are Better than Books

Molly Barton, co-founder of the new serialized reading experience Serial Box, tells us why original fiction is best digested in episodes.
BY MOLLY BARTON

The Giants of Xadin
by
Robert Locklear

Molly Barton loves books. She also loves TV. Since so much must-see-TV these days is being taken from books (see *The Handmaid's Tale*, *Game of Thrones*, *Big Little Lies*, *13 Reasons Why*, *American Gods*...), she thought "what if we make books more like TV?" Inspired by the Netflix and HBO lineups, she co-founded Serial Box, a website and iOS app that produces original fiction that reads like watching a TV show. Serials are written by a writer's room, and released in seasons of 13 episodes, just like a TV show. Weekly episodes pack a punch with only a 40-minute read-time or 60+-minute listen-time. The app even allows you to toggle back and forth between reading or listening.

One series the Read it Forward editors are addicted to: *Geek Actually*. *Geek Actually* is a sexy, geeky contemporary women's fiction series that follows the lives of five diverse, nerdy women as they navigate work, love, life, and the internet. For fans who love both *Sex and the City* as well as *Star Wars*, for anyone who knows that sci-fi can be sultry and that "gamer" is not gender-specific. We promise this serial will turn you on, rile you up, and leave you with five new friends.

- You can finish them!
  You all know the feeling—you climb into bed at the end of a long day and the book(s) you've been meaning to read are sitting there staring accusingly at you, unread, unloved. But somehow with your job and everything else going on in your life, you are managing to make time for your favorite hour-long tv shows (ahem, *GoT*) but not your to-read pile. Unlike a novel, the beauty of fiction serials is that every week a new episode is delivered to you and it takes just 40 minutes to read or about an hour to listen.

- Read in sync with friends
  Reading a serial your friends are also reading is like an ongoing book club without the annoying pressure to figure out who is going to host or whether to do a bar and how to split the bill. You can just pick a serial, figure out which of your friends are reading and

then chat about last week's episode in the course of your normal schedule. You can even gift a serial to a friend!

- Each episode stands on its own but there's a larger arc
I often think to myself, okay I am pressed for time but I want to read something really good during my commute or listen to something entertaining on my run. Podcasts are great but I also need a healthy dose of fiction to take my mind off the day to day. I find short stories frustrating—just when I've gotten into the voice of the writer and am rooting for the characters, it's over. Serial episodes provide a fully developed, satisfying story but are part of a larger story arc that's unfolding over the course of seasons so I know there's more story left for the next run.

- Sequels don't take forever to come out
I know George R. R. Martin is having a grand time working on the show but everyone is dying to read his next book. Single authored works can take a loooong time to come out. Serial Box has developed a highly unique team writing process built on my Penguin Random House editorial experience (with authors like Meg Rosoff, Nick Hornby, Anya Ulinich, Terry McMillan), my co-founder's theatre and gaming experience, and our work with TV writers. It doesn't hurt that my husband is a TV producer—he has helped us refine the process, and so have the 50+ writers we work with. We have figured out how to move quickly and maintain an extremely high quality of storytelling. We can bring out second and third seasons of our serials in 6-8 months.

- Hang out with characters you love every week
Much of the reason why I love shows like *Orange is the New Black* (also *Scandal* and *Suits*) is because I love spending time with the main characters every week—it's just a pleasure to see what they're up to. That is definitely the case in our newest series *Geek Actually,* which is sort of like *Sex and the City* but with nerdy diverse women who aren't all straight and who are friends online rather than in fancy cocktail bars. i09 called it "an ode to a generation of women who've figured out that they are not alone."

- Ditch what you don't like without over-committing
I've definitely had the experience where I've sampled a couple of pages from Amazon, thought that I liked it, bought it, and then found it went in a direction I really wasn't into. Serial Box gives fans free access (ebook and audio) to the full first episode of every series so you get almost an hour of content free before deciding if you want to subscribe and pay $1.59 for the next episode.

- Influence the story by being a vocal fan
I'll never forget how excited I was when I realized that the writers on the TV show *Fringe* were incorporating fan references into the show. Earlier this summer when Serial Box first launched the pilot episode of *Geek Actually* (called 'WTF' and written by lead writer Cathy Yardley) we held back the last few episodes of Season 1 before putting them through copy editing and audio recording because we wanted to see reader and listener reactions before we locked in the full season. Vocal fans on <u>Twitter</u>, <u>Facebook</u>, <u>and Instagram</u>or on our <u>blog</u> can influence the stories—we bring

dozens of pages of reader comments into our writers' rooms when we meet to work on new episodes.

- Switch back and forth between listening and reading (and we save your place)
  If you're a big reader and you commute on public transit, chances are you've had the heart-sinking moment when you get on the bus or train and realize there aren't any seats left so it's going to be tricky to pull out your book. Serial Box makes every series available in both e and audio, and our app makes it really easy to switch over to listening without losing your place, so you can keep right on going even when you have to strap-hang.

- Focus on representation – both in terms of characters and writers on the team
  To quote the awesome Shonda Rhimes, we are working to 'normalize' publishing in terms of characters on the page and writers at the keyboard. While it's not something we go around touting all the time, we are glad to see that fans and the press appreciate this focus—according to Autostraddle, *Tremontaine* is *"not just an entertaining series; it's an incisive cultural critique.... And it hurdles the Bechdel Test like a balance beam on a preschool playground."* And Den of Geek said, "the diversity of the [*Geek Actually]* cast is both wonderful and unsurprising given the writing team behind this serial."

- There's No I in Team
  Team writing draws off of every writers' strengths and lets them challenge each other to bring readers the best story possible. I would argue that team written serials are more entertaining than novels written by a single person alone because of the challenging and refining that goes on in the writers' room, and because of the strong focus on the reader/listener's experience while the story is being crafted. Nearly every time we've convened a writers' room for an in-person story summit, at some point during our long days together one of the writers exclaims "this process is like magic! It would've taken me 3 months to figure out that was a bad idea and we just solved it in 10 minutes of discussion!"

- Dickens for the smartphone age
  What do *The Three Musketeers, Anna Karenina,* and *The Pickwick Papers* have in common? Ding ding ding, they were all originally published in serial form in magazines or newspapers prior to being released in physical book form. The serial format is nothing new; we've just adapted it for the Netflix smartphone age and added audio.

MOLLY BARTON is the cofounder of Serial Box. Previously, Molly was the Head of Digital at Penguin Random House where she led the global eBook business, digital product innovation and content strategy. She previously founded Book Country, the writer collaboration and self-publishing platform. She earned her B.A. from Wesleyan University, where she has also served as a faculty member.

Marketing Books as an Indie Author
by Doug Dandridge

When you're an independent author, almost every job falls to you as the publisher of your work. There is no Marketing Department, no Public Relations, and no Distribution. As a self-published author, all of those jobs fall in my lap. I know some successful self-published authors who've hired people to set up their website, their blog, even their Twitter and Facebook accounts. I have not, so far, though if things keep picking up, I just might have to do that.

Pass The Carrots, Please
by
Donna M. Allen

Websites and blogs are not really all that difficult. There are programs that allow you to build a really nice website with point, click and drag. Same with blogs. I use WordPress, and it was relatively simple to set up. I was also able to get domain names that fit. My website is http://dougdandridge.net, while the blog is http://dougdandridge.com. Luckily, my last name is unusual enough that this works for me. For people with a more common last name, or the last name of an already famous personality, it can be more difficult. At first I tried to make the website as large as possible, which may have been a mistake, since a large website takes a lot of work to maintain, time I no longer have. The blog is much easier, and my blog is a large part of my marketing. I post at least once a week, sometimes more, depending on what is going on. I post about sci-fi and fantasy memes and tropes, movies, books, and especially about my own new releases, along with excerpts. I will also post how well my sales are doing, or reviews, or whatever. Partially, the blog is a way I communicate with fans, but it's also how I share with other writers what I am doing that works, and what doesn't. I post my blog on Twitter, my Facebook pages, and many specialty pages, both on Facebook, Google+ and Tumblr. This gives my blog a much larger reach than just my subscribers. I have hundreds of subscribers, but each blog gets thousands of views over time.

On Facebook I have both a personal page and an author's page, though the personal page gets a lot more traffic. If a fan wants to friend me, I always accept, and I regularly send requests to people I find interesting. Twitter is my heavy hitter. I started out, like everyone else, with very few followers. I joined the Independent Author's Network and started retweeting the tweets of other authors who had lots of followers. After a while I started tweeting my own stuff, and people with many more followers, some more than eighty thousand, retweeted me. Over time I started picking up followers, including some, like the Science Fiction Book Club, which, while they don't carry my work, is still an organization I am interested in knowing about me. Good publicity is always a good thing, if not with immediate returns, then eventual.

Goodreads was another useful resource. After signing on as an author, I discovered the books of mine they were already listing (which was a real rush). I then posted all of my books, my covers, excerpts, and book trailers. I found that the more venues I contacted, the better my chances of being discovered. The same with Shelfari, though they aren't as important as Goodreads.

From Honky Tonks
To
Churches

Vicki Lynn Smith

One of the more important things I did was to solicit reviews on Amazon. Not the pay for good reviews thing that some dishonest people try. I asked people I know who had read my books to give an honest review. I posted links in my ebooks to the sales page and asked for reviews. And then there were just the people who reviewed the books on their own. Somehow, I'm still not sure how, I have gotten over fourteen hundred reviews across all my books for a 4.5 star average. Some indies have more, and some have a lot better averages, but I'm satisfied with what I've gotten thus far.

Probably the biggest marketing boost I gave my books was doing a Kindle giveaway. The book has to be exclusive to Amazon, which causes some people problems. But I have sold a lot of books on that platform. I schedule the book for a freebie, normally the whole five days they allow every ninety. I went to the Author's Marketing Club site and used their free submission tool to alert a bunch of sites that my book would be free on those days. I also found a few others, as well as a bunch of Facebook pages that do the same thing. I blogged about the giveaway a couple of days before the start of the promotion, and tweeted it as well. I set up Hootsuite to tweet about twenty-five times a day so I could cover all time zones. On the day of the promotion I increased my own tweeting, and posted to every Facebook promotion page I could find. I also tweeted at twitter addresses that follow book giveaways. Three days into the promotion I did another blog post to inform people on how the promotion was coming, and to let them know the book was still available.

The first book I promoted this way was *The Deep Dark Well*, and I gave away 4,100 copies. Since then I have sold 5,500 copies of that book. I did giveaways of several other books that didn't do as well, either in the freebies or the later sales. But when I released *Exodus: Empires at War: Book 1* it flew off the Amazon hard drives. Later, book 2 of the series did the same, and that made my success. Some people say that the freebie promotion no longer works, but I ran a promotion on *Exodus: Empires at War: Book 1* and gave away 4,900 copies. The next month I sold more than five hundred copies of each of the five Exodus books already out, including book 1, and book 6 sold faster than any of the previous books in the series. Again, I went through all the steps I outlined above, and it really helped my overall sales for May, which (as of the date this post was written) was my best month ever.

When Amazon came out with Kindle Unlimited, I wasn't sure how that was going to impact my income. I made the decision to not put book 7 of the *Exodus* series with exclusivity to Amazon, even though Amazon is the only ebook seller it's listed on. I wanted to get people who were willing to buy the book do so first. The book sold just as fast as book 6. Another strategy I'm thinking of is publishing shorter works, in the 50,000 word range, and pricing them at about half the price of a novel.

As I said in the first paragraph, this is all on me. I have to make the decisions as to what I'm going to do. And each decision affects how much I make. *The Refuge* fantasy series is not making the money that *Exodus* is, but still has thousands of loyal fans. I've decided to keep the series going at this time, at least until I get to a logical stopping point. It just seems like the right thing to do, and I'm not hurting financially, so I can take a month and a half to write a book in that series every year. That's the wonderful thing about being an indie. I write what I want to write, and the books fit my own vision. The risk is that I succeed or fail by my own decisions, which may not be as well informed as that of a professional marketing department. But so far it's working.

•••

Doug Dandridge is a Florida native, Army veteran and ex-professional college student who spent way too much time in the halls of academia. He has worked as a psychotherapist, drug counselor, and, most recently, for the Florida Department of Children and Families. An early reader of Heinlein, Howard, Moorcock and Asimov, he has always had a love for the fantastic in books, TV and movies. Doug started submitting science fiction and fantasy in 1997 and collected over four hundred rejection letters. In December of 2011 he put his first self-publishing efforts online. Since then he had sold over 100,000 copies of his work, and has ranked in the top five on Amazon Space Opera and Military Science Fiction multiple times. He quit his day job in March 2013, and has since made a successful career as a self-published author.

Marketing tools for any self-published book

Paul Jarvis

The way you market your book should be based on two things: your values and the intentions for the book. If something feels slimy or inauthentic, don't do it. You should never let a bit of exposure trump your values. Short-term gains that feel wrong seldom result in long-term growth as an author. They can also decrease your **social capital**.

The intentions for your book can really be anything—credibility and status in your industry, increased bookings for speaking, consulting or projects, building your brand, further educating your audience with a new point of view on a subject they care about. Your book, your intentions. And however odd—because anyone can write a book now—books are still a strong signal that you're an expert on a topic or in a field.

If your intention is to sell a million copies or get on a best-seller list, that's more the result of many things going right, since it's really out of your control. Plus, most of the time, you're just going to be disappointed with that for a goal. Only a handful of books sell a million copies or get on the NYT or WSJ lists. And you don't need either to make money or build credibility (or even to have fun with your book).

A few of my books are "best-sellers" and it was really just a result of trying lots of things that slowly pushed sales higher. It's a war of attrition on experimenting, failing, learning, and continually pushing for more exposure and connections.

Your intentions also have to match the content and message of your book. For example, if you write a book about American Condors (which are EPIC, seriously), your intention can't really be to get more gigs speaking on the web design circuit. Or, if your book is about a super specific topic that relates to a teeny-weeny group of people, it'll never be a massive best-seller (but can definitely become a phenom in that small group).

It's all about them, not you
Once you've got an intention, move onto your audience. Who are they? Why will they care? Where do they currently get their information from?

If you don't know who your audience is, consider this:

1. Why did you write the book?

2. What do you want people to get from it?

3. Would people be motivated to get information from your book?

From there, think about what motivations people would have in common who would find that end result of your book valuable.

An audience of "everyone" is typically too big to grasp or connect with. Where does "everyone" get their information? There's no single source. What motivates "everyone" to learn something? There's no single motivation. What does "everyone" care about? There's no single topic.

You get the idea… "Everyone" is not your audience.
Your audience is a specific set of people with specific motivations and values. They're much easier to reach and connect with than everyone.

Your audience is probably awesome, but they are also self-serving and need to know what's in it for them (it's just human nature). What are they going to learn that can't be found anywhere else? How will they benefit from this knowledge? How can they apply that knowledge to better their lives, careers, or wallets? They're putting both their money and their time into the book, so they need to be sure it's worth both. Even free books have a large investment of someone's time.

Meet your audience where they hang out

Once you have a handle on your audience and what motivates them, you've got to go to them. Where are they currently getting their information? Which blogs, podcasts, publications, influencers, and media outlets do they consume?

Make a list that includes contacts at each source. Their name, email address, and social media profiles. Then start to follow them, interact with them in a way that fits with you, help if they ask any questions or need assistance. Get on their radars. Keep notes about your interactions.

If it's a publication that accepts guest posts, start pitching them. If it's a podcast, ask to be a guest. If it's a blog that does interviews, ask to be interviewed. In each instance, lead with what's in it for them and their audience. Also, keep notes on which people you've pitched, and if they accepted or turned you down (so you don't pitch the same person the same idea twice).

Not many people are going to promote you and your book out of the goodness of their hearts, unless you've built strong relationships with them first. It's better to pitch yourself and your book on how it relates to their audience and how it will benefit their audience. Just like figuring out the motivations of your audience in order to sell books, you've got to figure out the motivations of the sources your audience consumes to pitch what's in it for them to feature you.

Marketing tools

As I said at the start, there's no single way to market a book that's guaranteed to fit with your personality and also have massive results. What you can do is align your book with your intentions and values, and constantly work at moving in that direction.

Selling your book and selling what's in your book is the same. You wrote a book because you wanted to convince people of an idea. Marketing your book is really just convincing people that the idea is worth the purchase price and time to read it.

The tools you use to market aren't just creative or design decisions; they're marketing choices that need to align with your intentions and your audience.

These are tools you need to have in place to launch any marketing plan:

Book title

What are you delivering in the content? Is the title easy to remember? Is it both descriptive and captivating? If necessary to explain the premise more, use a byline to push just a little more information on the cover. Use it to narrow down your audience (who it's for, who it's not for), get more specific or describe the key point.

Book story

What story are you telling with your book in 1–2 sentences? Use this for pitches to media, your mailing list, or as the call to action on your site. Why is the story interesting? Test different one-sentence stories on social media (and measure the resulting clicks) or on your newsletter (using A/B tests). Adapt your story based on what performs best. Your story is how you describe your book in writing or in interviews.

Cover

Does it look professional? This is the biggest factor. Because anyone can publish a book, you don't want your cover to look like you made it yourself (unless you're a pro book cover designer). It has to look as good or better than the biggest books in your category.

Author bio

You need three of these: one sentence (for things like social media bios), one paragraph (for bylines on guest posts), and one page (for all the details). Include your relevant accomplishments, relevant credentials, previous books, press mentions ("as seen in X"), and anything interesting that your audience will think is interesting, too. If you have a hard time writing something that balances being criminally egotistical and not boastful enough, ask a friend, editor, or reader to help write it. Sometimes it's easier for someone else to talk about you than it is for you to talk about yourself.

Author photo

For self-published books, you want more professional and less Instagram selfie. Use a pro camera or hire a professional to make sure you've got a photo that looks as good or better than the top authors, and also matches the style of your writing (if it's casual writing, wear a t-shirt, if it's formal, wear a suit or sleek black dress, etc.). Make sure your face is the biggest part and the focal point of the shot. Save your creativity for your next poetry-slam.

Book description
You also need three of these: one sentence, one paragraph, and one page. This is less a summary of the content and more the sales pitch on why someone needs to read it. What's interesting, noteworthy, or newsworthy about it? What's the most important thing your audience will learn? Why should anyone care that you wrote it? What is the benefit of reading it?

Mailing list
Hands down the most useful tool, however you use it, is your mailing list. Start collecting emails before your book is ready (with a coming soon landing page), use it as an announcement list when your book is ready, and use it to consistently communicate with your audience. There's no better way for an author to talk to their audience and sell books than a newsletter.

The grand finale
These tools are all opportunities to sell your book using whatever marketing method you feel resonates the most with you and your audience. Your choices on cover, title, blurb, and bio all need to be carefully crafted with your audience in mind.

The key—the absolute key—to marketing a book is to have written a great book that people actually want to read and then talk about. Then it's a matter of figuring out what aligns with your intentions in terms of getting the word out.

Write for your audience, not for yourself (even if it's a memoir). If the quality doesn't happen within the pages of the book, no amount of marketing is going to help in the long run (even if you pay for it).

Books are sold by word-of-mouth and regular people talking to other regular people about what they read. Press and publicity help, but the best promotion comes from people telling the people they know to read something. Write something worth reading and worth gushing about. Is it difficult to do? Totally. It requires lots of work, revisions, editing and testing. If it is impossible to do? Hell no.

Less convincing and hard selling needs to happen if people can easily grasp your concept and want to get your insight on your chosen topic. So be clear, be useful, and be unique.

Have all of the above in place well before you launch your book. Plan out exactly how you're going to market your book, using the tools above as laser-focused weapons to slice through the existing noise of everyone else's self-published book.

Self-published romance ebooks top the sales list

An Interesting Marketing Report:

<u>Smashwords have released their annual ebook survey</u>, and it is quite startling to discover how dominant self-published romance novels have become. In short, the romance genre accounts for a staggering 87% of the top 100 bestsellers on Smashwords and their aggregators. Should I repeat that number? Eighty-seven percent!

While it is impossible to compare this data with sales of self-published romance novels on Amazon Kindle, one could make a logical assumption that romance probably also dominates Kindle ebook sales.

However, with such a clear dominance of one genre making up such a massive proportion of ebook sales by Smashwords, where does this leave writers of other genres? This could explain why some authors of genres other than romance, erotica and YA often find it difficult to gain sales traction on Smashwords.

Letters to My Father in Law
Whom I have never met
By
Julia C. Huncycutt

After romance, the top selling genres are headed by erotica and YA, with Literary fiction just managing to make it into Smashwords' top fiction genres.

<u>Romance ebooks account for 70% of to 10 bestsellers</u>

Not only are self-published romance novels dominating Smashwords' sales, they are still increasing in percentage terms. Up from 70% in 2014 to 87% in 2015. The note on the slide below makes for interesting reading, however. The description of the smartest authors in the business may well be true, but it misses one extremely relevant criteria. They must also write romance! It seems to matter little from the data if an author is organized, professional, sophisticated or experimental unless you write romance you have little chance of success

Categories of Top 100 Bestselling Smashwords Books

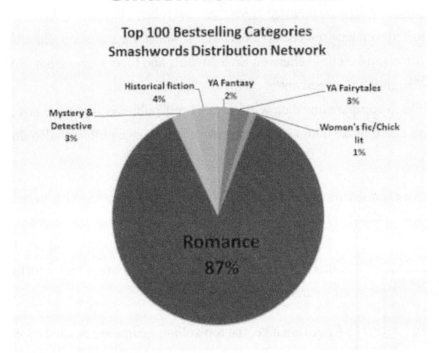

So what does all this data mean to self-publishing authors?

Smashwords have an ebook catalogue of about 400,000 compared to Kindle at around 4 million, so in many respects, it is difficult to compare the two retail platforms. However, from the data they have released, it may explain why many authors struggle to sell ebooks on Smashwords. Simply put, you write in the wrong genre for ebook buyers, who are buying their ebooks from Smashwords and their aggregators, Apple, B&N and Kobo.

I know from my own experience that I have never had much success on Smashwords, even though my ebooks sell quite well and steadily on Kindle. Writing self-published romance novels is certainly not my cup of tea, as science fiction farce, speculative fiction and literary fiction are the genres I prefer to write. There is no way in the world I could possibly write romance.

So success on Smashwords seems to be, not how well you write, but what you write.

I know there has been a lot of discussion about self-publishing on the available platforms to Indie authors, with a range of views about the relative sales success on each platform. There is also, of course, the debate about <u>open publishing</u> and making ebooks available to readers on as many platforms as possible, as opposed to exclusivity on Amazon.

However, with this sales data released by Smashwords, it would seem to me that if you are not an author of self-published romance novels, you are probably not having a lot of sales success with Smashwords. But at least you now know why. You may write very well, but not in one of their popular and saleable genres.

The Author Bio
Is an Important Marketing Tool

Posted by CreateSpaceBlogger on Sep 27, 2010 11:25:56 AM

The author biography is oftentimes the last item we think about as self-published authors. As a result, we may even consider it to be the least important part of our marketing strategy. It's fluff, words to fill in space, right? No, not by a long shot. In many ways, it can be as important as your one-sentence pitch, and it is a key component for you to build your personal brand.

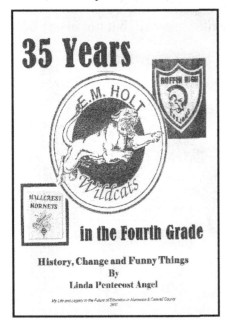

I've developed a few author bios as my career and experience progressed. And looking over them with a critical eye, my very first bio was my most successful. It was short out of necessity, because I didn't bring a lot to the table in the way of credentials. It was for my first book and all I had going for me at the time was that my family claimed to really like it. I knew enough to know that wasn't a great selling point. I sat down and wrote bio after bio trying to make myself sound a lot more important than I really was. The harder I tried, the less authentic the bio read. After literally hours of trying and failing, I set the project aside and walked through my house, trying to figure out who I was. I patted my dog for inspiration. I made sure that cats had food. I flipped through the mail and rolled my eyes at a mortgage statement. I stared at my wedding picture on the mantel, and that's when it hit me. This is who I am. I'm just a regular guy who wants you to read my book. So, I wrote the following bio:

Linda Pentecost. Angel from Burlington, North Carolina caught my attention with her book titled, "35 years in the Fourth Grade.". Her bio mentions the more 1000 students she taught during her career. One has to believe the former students and their families will be interested in her book.

That was it. I added it to the back cover, and didn't give it another thought. An odd thing started happening. I got e-mails from people telling me they loved my bio. I'd show the book to people at book fairs and signing events, and they'd flip the book over, read the bio, and laugh. They'd walk off with a copy of the book based on the bio. The book has now been on the market for five years, and I still get remarks about the bio. This one was even posted in a recent review:

For that ugly mortgage
Haven't read it yet, but the "ugly mortgage" comment gave me a giggle

I changed my bio for later books because I felt it needed to include information about awards I had won and other books I had published, but I've never received a single comment about those. Credentials are important and include them whenever possible, especially if you're writing as an expert on the topic of the book, but don't use that as an excuse not to connect with your readers.

What's the lesson? Write the bio in third person, but take the opportunity to let it reflect your personality. And by all means, keep it short.

Richard Ridley is an award-winning author and paid CreateSpace contributor.

Where and How to Sell Your Poetry Books

Denise Enck

So, you've self-published your book. Now what?

Your book just arrived from the printer. Having them published was the easy part. Now your greatest challenge is upon you – you need to get your work out of those boxes and into the hands of appreciative readers.

It's difficult enough for publishers to sell poetry books (poetry sells slowly & people are especially hesitant to buy books by unknown poets), so marketing your own is a big challenge. Here are my suggestions for selling your book either online or off.

What are the qualities of poetry books which sell well?

I've found, through experience in selling poetry books (especially self-published books, or those by little-known poets) both on the Empty Mirror site & in brick-and-mortar bookstores, and through the experiences of my poet clients, that poetry books really only sell if 4 conditions are met:

- The work must be of high quality.
- The price must be reasonable and the book must be nicely produced.
- If selling online, sample poems must be provided.
- The poet works actively at self-promotion (online & off), letting people know where the books can be purchased.

The unfortunate fact is that if any of these conditions are not met, the books will likely sit unsold.

Pondering
A Collection of Lyrical Poems and Epigrams
By
Beth Shockley Canada

A note on expectations

Remember, even in mainstream publishing, there's a small market for poetry books. Even established poets don't sell thousands of books – maybe not even hundreds. More people will read for free (online, in a periodical, or flipping through a printed book) than will buy the book.

For example, I know of one very well-known poet whose collections have been published by major publishers & literary presses for decades; a recent collection was published in an edition of just 600 copies.

Another highly-regarded poet's work was published in a chapbook in an edition of 300 copies, and a couple dozen still remain unsold nearly 8 years later. And, he'd had books published – by both small & major presses – for over 40 years.

That's not unusual. Many poetry books – even by famous poets – are published in limited editions of as little as 26 lettered copies, with numbered editions 100 or 200 being fairly common.

While some books by high-profile poets do sell many thousands, that's quite a rare exception in the poetry world, and one reserved for an elite few who have built a reputation over many years (such as Maya Angelou, Allen Ginsberg, or perhaps U.S. Poet Laureates such as Donald Hall or Billy Collins).

So, please keep your expectations reasonable. Even if your book is terrific & you do everything right, you may not sell thousands — or even hundreds — of books or make a lot of money. That's OK, it's just the reality of the current market for poetry in this country.

Where to sell your poetry books

OK! So, you've got your book ready to sell & you've got the energy to promote it. Great! You can market your book either online or offline.

Sell offline:

It's *much* easier to sell your books offline than online, because folks will have an opportunity to leaf through the book and read as many poems as they like before purchasing.

Try local independent bookstores to see if they will buy a few, or (most likely) take a few copies on consignment. (The big chain bookstores will not be able to do this; their buyers in New York do all the buying and don't buy self-published books.)

other shops

If there are local gift shops or other retail establishments you regularly frequent, ask them if they would be willing to take a few.

See if you can arrange a book signing at a bookstore, or another local venue (a club? a grocery store?)

If you participate in local poetry readings, take a few books along to sell after your reading.

Sell online:

Why not have your own website? Sell your books on your own website (it's easy to do.) You can also put the address on your business cards, trade links with other poets. Other online selling & marketing techniques are most effective when you have your own website, too. If your book is published by a self-publishing or print-on-demand type of publisher, they may sell the book on their website, or market it for you. (See the self-publishing link above.)

Try Amazon.com. They do sell self-published books, <u>complete their online application</u> to get started.

eBay.com

eBay is easy to use and can be an effective way to sell your book.

Ideas for promoting your poetry book

Regardless of where you sell your books – online or off – you're going to have to tirelessly promote yourself. Poetry books – and other self-published books – don't sell unless you really make some noise & bring attention to yourself. Even then, it's tough.

Promote your book (offline):

See if the local newspaper will write an article about you. (The little local weeklies that are distributed for free are a good bet.)

Put up flyers on bulletin boards at your school, library, church, grocery store, work, etc. Leave business cards everywhere.

Send out press releases to local newspapers, newsletters & bookshops. (Don't send free review copies unless you are absolutely certain they will review it. Most reviewers / booksellers disregard unsolicited review copies.)

Set up a reading (and/or a book signing) at a local cafe, bookshop, gallery, school, college, church, fraternal organization, library, or another local gathering place. Do it alone, or recruit some other local poets (or musicians) for a bigger crowd & more sales opportunities. Create an event!

Get published in literary magazines & other publications. (See our publishing advice page to find out how.)

Tell all your previous publishers (perhaps literary magazines & other periodicals) where your books can be purchased (& your web address, if you have one). Ask if they'd be interested in reviewing your book. Maybe ask if they'd like a review copy. They may publish information about how your book can be purchased. If not, consider placing a small advertisement in their publication. Since they published you, their readers may be your best bet for sales.

Participate in open mike poetry reading nights.

Is there a local radio show that would like to interview you?

Does the local library have regular readings or programs in which you can participate? (Or, as suggested above, perhaps you can schedule your own reading. Ask the manager.)

Keep a copy or two of your book with you (in your car, or bag…) in case you run into someone who's interested.

Have business cards made & give them out to everyone, put them on bulletin boards, have them available at poetry readings.

Promote your book online:

These techniques work best if you have your own website.

If you don't have your own website, <u>learn about getting one</u>. (It doesn't have to be expensive! The owner of Empty Mirror, Denise,

designs <u>affordable, effective custom websites for writers</u>.)

Other online promotion techniques are much more effective if you also have your own website.

Whether you have your own website or not, send a press release to online magazines, literary websites, and reviewers who may be interested in your book.

Put your website's address (or, the web addresses of websites that sell your work) in your email signature.

If you participate in online forums, newsgroups, or blogs, use your web address in your signature (if permitted).

Social networking sites are free, easy to work with, and let you connect easily with readers and other writers. You can share photos, your written words, and blog posts. Twitter, Facebook, Pinterest, and LinkedIn are the big ones.

If you have your own website, get links from related websites (other writers, publishers, literary websites, sites about your topic). Link to high-quality related websites as well. Most people will find your website through links and search engines (which rely on links), so this is very critical to your site's success.

Keep your website current – add new information at least once a month. This will keep your readers (& the search engines) coming back. Add a poem, essay, review, some news or reading dates, etc.

Purchase advertising on search engines, directories, & sites relating to your topic. Options are available for any budget. Some websites may even be willing to trade ads with you.

One good place to look into advertising is Google Adwords, as it has a very wide reach.

For more ideas on promoting your website online, see my <u>website promotion advice</u>. Or, <u>email me (Denise)</u> – I'd be glad to help with advice or services. (I do this for a living.)

Get Your Own Website

Having your own website can be a very useful tool in selling books. It allows you to tell your potential readers a bit about yourself, publish sample poems from your book, and tell folks where they can buy it. (You can even sell your book through the website.) You can share photos, links, and recent news and tell everyone about upcoming events. You can add a mailing list, message board, or blog (or, the entire site can be set up as a blog).

The site would be findable on Google and the other search engines for relevant searches. Having your own website gives you a professional image and can be invaluable in marketing yourself and your work.

We are very experienced in designing websites for writers and other creative people; we've been doing it since 2000. For more information on our services, please see:

- <u>Quanta Web design for the Arts</u>
  This is our web design business. The site offers complete information about what we offer, and a full design portfolio.

- <u>Email Denise</u> Got questions? Want to get started? Whatever your need, I'd be glad to help!

What are some helpful websites on the topic of marketing self-published books?

- <u>Amazon.com Advantage book sales application</u>
- <u>ISBN.org</u> You'll need an ISBN (book ID number / bar code) to sell books to most bookstores & to Amazon, etc.
- <u>Book marketing resources</u> a gold mine of information!
- <u>101 Book marketing websites</u>
- <u>Advice on getting your book reviewed.</u>

I hope this information is helpful & not discouraging. It certainly takes a lot of work to market a self-published book – but once you've gotten your poems out into the world you'll undoubtedly find that it's worthwhile! If you'd like to hire me to build a website for you, or to promote the one you've got – or if you'd just like to chat – feel free to <u>get in touch with me</u>.

Denise Enck is Empty Mirror's editor. She's <u>edited</u> several other literary magazines and small-press publications since the 1980s. When not at Empty Mirror, you can find her writing, making collages, traveling the Pacific Northwest, or working at <u>Quanta Web Studio</u>.

How to Pitch And Sell A Movie Based On Your Autobiography Or Life Story

Life in The House By The Creek

Charlie Wilson
Burlington, North Carolina

There are ways to get a movie made about your autobiography. However, it's an uphill battle. Let me share some tactics you can use when pitching your autobiography or memoir.

A difficult aspect of selling your autobiography is that you can lose perspective. When people accept or reject aspects of your autobiography, it's easy to take it personally.

Therefore, to have the best chance to get your autobiography published or produced, you need to be able to see the pluses and minuses of the project in a more objective way.

Imagine how someone you don't know would pitch your autobiography.

- How would they start?
- What elements would they highlight?
- What would they leave out?
- How would they describe YOU?

Most decision-makers are suspicious of people who are pitching autobiographical projects. This is because there are a lot of people who believe "my life should be a movie/book," when their life isn't the kind of story that would interest a large audience.

One of the best ways to sell your autobiography is to partner with someone known for working with biographical material, and let them pitch it. That provides a crucial ingredient to getting a decision-maker interested: third-party validation.

The single best thing you can do to make a decision-maker see the value of your autobiography is to convince other decision-makers that it is valuable.

For example:

- Get a story about you written in the local paper.
- Get a national magazine to feature you.
- Attach a producer who specializes in biography.
- Attach a star to the project who wants to play "you."

What Is The 'Movie Story' Version Of Your Autobiography?

Thinking about what your autobiography would look like as a movie can help you clarify the most compelling aspects of the project. This will help you to pitch it effectively (whether you want it to be a movie or not).

Movies need to have a simple, clear story that maximizes visual interest. This often requires making significant adjustments to the actual events of your life. That's why real lives and movie versions often differ.

If your story was going to be a movie, how would you have to shape or adjust your story to fit the medium?

See Your Autobiography From The Decision-Maker's POV

Autobiographies, whether a book like *Lucky Man* (by and about Michael J. Fox), a movie like *8 Mile* (about and starring Eminem), or a TV show like *Louie* (by, about, and starring Louis C.K.) have lots of potential to make money.

However, decision-makers such as agents, executives, and publishers typically do not want to invest in an autobiography unless it meets at least one of two standards:

1. It must be incredible, timely, and relevant.
2. It must already be successful in some other medium.

You may have an unusual, amazing life story. But if it is not also timely and relevant to what's happening in our culture, decision-makers are unlikely to want to invest.

To develop a more compelling pitch for your project:

- Identify famous historical analogues to your story.
- Link your story to trends in contemporary culture.
- Reference current news stories on the same topic.

Here are two autobiographies that are in development. I've chosen them because neither author is a celebrity though both have extraordinary stories.

- American Sniper, by Chris Kyle
- A Long Way Home, by Saroo Brierly

Something to notice about these two examples—neither was sold immediately as a movie. *American Sniper* was a successful book first, and Saroo Brierly's story received significant international press coverage, then was sold as a book to Penguin and as a movie to See-Saw Films (*The King's Speech*).

This demonstrates one of the key ingredients of selling your autobiography: **proving that it has been successful in another medium.**

Already Successful In Another Medium

If you are a celebrity, this is a form of success in another medium. Being a famous actor, businessperson, or other "star" is one kind of evidence that there may be a market for material about YOU.

So, for example, an autobiography in development is:

- <u>Foxy, My Life In Three Acts,</u> by Pam Grier

However, if you're not a celebrity, there are other ways to prove that your story is worth telling. Here are some things I have seen people do that helped them to sell an autobiographical project:

- Getting national press
- Performing a financially successful one-person show
- Distributing a short film on YouTube which goes viral
- Creating a popular blog about your life
- Publishing articles that leverage your experience
- Becoming a public speaker

How To Use Your Personal Story

This may surprise you, but if you're pitching an autobiography, this is what you should do:

If possible, pitch the project without referencing yourself at all.

Prove that the story stands on its own. Then, if you get sufficient interest from the decision-maker and you get asked how you came up with the idea, with humility and brevity you can describe the part of your own life that gave rise to the project.

This strategy is more effective than leading with your connection to the material because:

1. You demonstrate professionalism by showing that the story comes first.
2. Your personal connection adds credibility to the material.
3. Your personal experience acts as a "button" to an already strong pitch.

Written by Stephanie Palmer

Stephanie Palmer was a film executive with MGM Pictures and The Hollywood Reporter named her one of the "Top 35 Executives Under 35." She is the author of the best-selling book Good in a Room. She has helped many writers get agents and managers…

Sexist violence sickens crime critic

Leading novelist says graphic depictions of sadistic misogyny have become so extreme she refuses to review some new fiction

@byamaliahill

Crime fiction has become so violently and graphically anti-women that one of the country's leading crime writers and critics is refusing to review some violent new books.

Jessica Mann, an award-winning author who reviews crime fiction for the *Literary Review*, has said that an increasing proportion of the books she is sent to review feature male perpetrators and female victims in situations of "sadistic misogyny". "Each psychopath is more sadistic than the last and his victims' sufferings are described in detail that becomes ever more explicit, as young women are imprisoned, bound, gagged, strung up or tied down, raped, sliced, burned, blinded, beaten, eaten, starved, suffocated, stabbed, boiled or buried alive," she said.

"Authors must be free to write and publishers to publish. But critics must be free to say they have had enough. So however many more outpourings of sadistic misogyny are crammed on to the bandwagon, no more of them will be reviewed by me," said Mann, who has written her own bestselling series of crime novels and a non-fiction book about female crime writers.

She said that when a female corpse recently appeared on the jacket of a crime-writing colleague's new book, the author pointed out to her publisher that the victim in the story was actually a man. Mann said the publisher replied: "Never mind that. Dead, brutalized women sell books, dead men don't. Nor do dead children or geriatrics."

Mann said the most disturbing plots were by female authors. "The trend cannot be attributed to an anti-feminist backlash because the most inventive fiction of this kind is written by women," she claimed. "They are, one author explained to me, best qualified to do so because girls grow up knowing that being female is 'synonymous with being prey'." The British market for crime fiction is worth more than £116m a year, with almost 21 million books sold. Women account for almost 60% of the genre's market, with females aged over 55 the most avid readers.

Natasha Cooper, former chair of the Crime Writers' Association, agreed with Mann. "There is a general feeling that women writers are less important than male writers and what can save and propel them on to the bestseller list is if they produce at least one novel with very graphic violence in it to establish their credibility and prove they are not girly," she said.

Val McDermid, author of the books adapted for the television series *Wire in the Blood* starring Robson Green, whose novel *The Mermaids Singing* won the association's Gold Dagger for best crime novel of the year, said that crime writing was increasingly "sensationalist and gratuitous" because of the demands of the market.

"There has been a general desensitization among readers, who are upping the ante by demanding ever more sensationalist and gratuitous plotlines," she said. "But when women write about violence against women, it will almost inevitably be more terrifying because women grow up knowing that to be female is to be at risk of attack. We write about violence from the inside. Men, on the other hand, write about it from the outside."

Selina Walker, publishing director for crime at Transworld, denied that women wrote more graphically violent books than men. The best crime writing, she said, could be "viewed as female wish-fulfilment".

"Readers like to be vicariously frightened by stories of what's going on in the wicked world outside but closure is always a total given," she said. "The sales figures of authors such as Tess Gerritsen, Mo Hayder, Karin Slaughter and Kathy Reichs would indicate that female readers enjoy reading scary novels – and in impressive numbers."

How to become an ebook superstar

Ben Galley, a self-published author of fantasy books also offers a consultancy service for would-be writers.

@patrick_barkham

It has never been easier to publish your own book. Traditional publishers may take a year to turn your manuscript into print on a page but you can get your own ebook on sale around the world in about four minutes. The real battle, however, is the same as it ever was: how do you find an audience?

Old-school publishing houses will almost certainly endure. Their expertise in not only editing but distributing and publicizing your book increases its chances of success. But alongside them are a growing number of authors who have become editor/designer/marketeer/sales director for their own ebooks. In return for this slog, instead of a modest advance plus 8%–15% royalty from a traditional publisher, a self-published author may enjoy royalties of 70% if their book is sold at a certain price (£1.49 to £7.81) in the Kindle store. Self-published authors will also get the buzz

Selected Writings
Some Stories, Mostly Short and Mostly True
By
Jerry M. Whitmire

of seeing their ebooks in high-street shops after Waterstones recently made a surprise deal with rival Amazon to sell Kindles and its ebooks through its 300 stores.

1. Choose the right book, the right genre and the right title

"Write for the right reasons – ie yourself," says Kerry Wilkinson, the 31-year-old sports journalist from Preston who became Britain's bestselling ebook author – beating established megasellers such as Lee Child and Stieg Larsson – on Amazon in the final quarter of last year. "If I had set out to sell tens of thousands of copies and sign with a publisher, then I would likely have ended up achieving nothing because I would have been focused on the wrong things," he says.

If the book you have written for yourself is a delicate work of literary fiction, a children's book or an esoteric subject (butterflies, say), it may be better to persevere with attracting a mainstream publisher. At this stage in the digital revolution, the successful self-published ebooks spring from popular genres, and those for which there are already big online communities – fantasy, erotica, chick-lit, horror and crime thrillers. Be careful with your title: in an era of keywords, tags and search engine optimisation, it has never been more important. Distinctive is good; baffling, however, is not. According to a recent survey by the Sydney-based Taleist blog, self-published romance authors earn the most – 170% more than their peers.

2. Don't just rely on Twitter or Facebook

Ben Galley became a self-published author at 22 and is currently making a modest living selling his fantasy ebooks and offering "Shelf Help", a consultancy for other aspiring authors (sessions via Skype, phone or face to face from £50 to £199). He believes every author must create a website. "Some people survive off Twitter or a blog, but you need an online presence. Most people who buy your book want to find out more about you and they can't find that from your Twitter feed," he says. "A website is a sales platform, it's a marketing platform and it's a global presence if you do it right." He recommends building one with iWeb if you have a Mac, but customizable blog platforms created through Tumblr or Wordpress can work as well.

Wilkinson agrees: "I set up a website with information about future releases and that has provided more publicity for me than Twitter and Facebook combined."

3. Crowd-source some help

Steven Lewis, a writer and blogger for the Taleist, produced its fascinating survey of more than 1,000 self-published authors last month.

It shows that self-publishers who take the most professional approach to production – getting external help (editors, proofreaders and, especially, cover designers) – make on average 34% more from their books. "Self-publishing is a triathlon," says Lewis. "Writing your book might feel like a marathon but it's just the first leg. The second leg is the production, and the third is marketing. Readers care deeply about things such as formatting and proofreading. If you have been sloppy, they will mention it in the reviews and it will hurt your sales." Help need not be expensive: Ben Galley crowd-sourced his cover design (for a small fee) and even persuaded readers to proofread his second novel. The average production spend is £440.

4. Go high-risk

Rachel Abbott, the retired former boss of an interactive media company, became an Amazon No 1 bestseller this year with her psychological thriller Only the Innocent. Sales took off after she designed a marketing plan that focused on Amazon. "Amazon is all about visibility. I looked at the ways your book could be made visible and exploited those opportunities," she says. When buyers browse genres in Amazon, they can list books by average review. Some authors get friends and family to post positive reviews, but readers soon smell a rat when they see these reviewers have never judged another book. Abbott took the "high-risk" approach of sending a review request document to bloggers who wrote about thrillers (only choose relevant bloggers). Just like any job application or sales pitch, a personalized request is most persuasive; so is one including details about your book and links to any previous reviews, Twitter feeds and websites to whet the bloggers' appetites. Offers of interviews or guest blogs may also encourage bloggers to publicize your book.

For Abbott, good reviews boosted her book's visibility on Amazon.

5. Give it away. Now!

Everyone loves a freebie, especially online. Kenny Scudero, a 22-year-old from New York, says offering his ebook debut, Comfortably Awkward, for free on Kindle one weekend was the best marketing method he used.

"I wouldn't say it's definitely required," says Galley, but it also worked for him. He gave away his debut novel, The Written, for a month last August. Before his giveaway, he was selling roughly 50 copies per week; afterwards, his sales more than doubled, and stayed high. "The free charts on Amazon are constantly trawled by people with voracious reading appetites," he says. Getting read is an obvious way to sell more copies via word of mouth – if your book is any good. For authors wanting to eat, giveaways should be for a limited time only.

6. Use social media in a clever way

Even the dimmest celebrity has grasped that Twitter is a great way to sell themselves. But a recent Verso survey estimated that barely 12% of books are discovered from social networks whereas 50% are passed on via personal recommendations.

Everyone is a bit hazy about how best to use social media but there are specific ways of finding an audience. Abbott purchased a piece of marketing software called Tweet Adder that enabled her to make contact with people who followed other authors in the same genre.

7. Talk, don't spam

Spamming strangers via Twitter is not usually a route to sales success. Self-published authors and gurus still see too many authors conducting one-way shouting about their book. "Be interesting, be generous, and be interested in others," is Lewis's advice. "The principle is to be human," advises Galley. Chat about stuff other than your book, reply to everyone, and don't get drawn into slanging matches with hostile reviewers. "A lot of writers make a mistake by going on Twitter and spending all their time spamming people saying 'buy my book'. I don't do too much of that," says Wilkinson.

Building an audience on Twitter is time-consuming. How often is it OK to plug your book? "I recommend sending out promotional tweets maybe once an hour, but not more than every 30 minutes," says US self-published sci-fi author Michael Hicks online. Once an hour?! Galley suggests five times – a day. That sounds like a full-time job to me – try employing your sulky teenager or dog to do it for you.

8. Be ready to slave away

Working through the night to write a book while slaving away at a menial day job is an obligatory component of every romantic self-published success story. Anyone who has knocked out 70,000 words on top of a job and family life doesn't need to be told to work hard. What is new, perhaps, is that this nocturnal drudgery doesn't stop with your book's publication. Galley gets up at 7am to do what he calls his "social media rounds", visiting eight or nine different social media sites to keep abreast of online chatter. As any author promoting a book knows, promotional duties play havoc with writing. Unlike many authors, Galley stays online even when he is writing. "I always make sure I can see the Twitter screen on my laptop when I am writing," he says. He claims the quality of his work is not affected. If only it was true for all of us. Too much marketing may be a damaging distraction: according to the Taleist survey, top earners all spent more time writing than marketing their books.

9. Take it to a bookshop

The fusty old book business may still be a lifeline for self-published authors and its collapse hurts all authors. The online world that opens so many doors is shutting others. Ian Collins, an arts journalist and author, recently wrote of how a book he published through a small imprint about the artists of Southwold sold 1,300 copies in two bookshops in the Suffolk coastal town. He and his small publisher would love to reprint but Southwold's two bookshops have now closed down. There is no marketplace for his book except online, where it is being offered for £85 plus postage on Amazon's marketplace (none of which will go to Collins or his publisher). Self-published authors with books that serve a particular geographical audience can find audiences through bookshops – where they still exist. The physical book is expensive to self-publish but it can still be worth it, if you can persuade a sympathetic outlet to stock it. Offer it on a sale-or-return basis, and give them a generous (40%) margin if you can.

10. Aim higher

The future may be a world where authors prove themselves in the self-published world before they are snapped up by mainstream publishers. Self-published success invariably leads to big book deals. Should authors swap 70% royalties for a traditional deal? "Initially I was definitely better off self-publishing. I've built an audience, plus made friends and money I never would have done through a publisher," says Wilkinson, who has now signed a six-book deal with Pan Macmillan. "Sales of physical books are still higher than ebooks, so there was always likely to be a point where I could do with some help. I had nothing to lose by taking a publishing deal."

John Locke, the self-published American millionaire, has also branched out into physical books, but says he has done it a different way: he has signed a distribution deal (not a publishing deal – Locke says he still controls his product) with Simon & Schuster so that his self-published book, Wish List, can get into shops across the US and Canada.

"My distribution agreement, if successful, could lead to many more such deals between trade publishers and indie authors and demonstrates a way for indies to finally make it into bookstores and receive interviews and reviews from mainstream media," Locke says online.

And finally ... the dirty secret

No, not erotica, although that's not a bad idea – the print version of EL James's originally self-published Fifty Shades of Grey sold 100,000 copies in its first week in the UK, becoming the fastest-selling book this year.

Is it a coincidence that many successful self-published authors have had web-based careers? "The wonderful thing about self-publishing is that it is a level playing field," says Lewis. "If there is a 'secret', it's only that being a self-publisher today means you are an online marketer." Self-publishers should teach themselves online marketing, he recommends, from sites such as Copyblogger.

One secret is that despite the tempting royalty slices available, you almost certainly won't make much money. Half of the self-published authors in the Taleist survey earned less than £320 in 2011 from their books; 75% of reported revenues were concentrated among less than 10% of authors. Those who had an agent earned three times their unrepresented peers.

Wilkinson's day job involves web journalism but his success, he insists, was the same as any book throughout history: his book found an audience via word-of-mouth. "The truth is, there is no magic wand. Regardless of anyone who tries to flog you a 'How to sell a million books' guide, it is the dirty secret no one will share – a lot of it is luck."

The National Book Awards
Make a Powerful Statement

ARNAV ADHIKARI

The Atlantic Dailey, a free weekday email newsletter

When John Lewis took the stage Wednesday night to accept the National Book Award for Young People's Literature for his graphic novel *March: Book Three*, the congressman was on the verge of tears. The book, co-authored with Andrew Aydin and illustrated by Nate Powell, is the final installment in the trilogy that follows the civil rights movement through the eyes of Lewis, who was at its heart. "This is unbelievable … some of you know I grew up in rural Alabama, very poor, very few books in our home," Lewis said, his voice shaking. "I remember in 1956, when I was 16 years old, going to the public library to get library cards, and we were told the library was for whites only and not for coloreds. And to come here and receive this honor, it's too much."

It was a powerful moment that set the tone for the ceremony, which went on to see three out of four of its categories won by African American authors (the Poetry award went to Daniel Borzutzky for *The Performance of Becoming Human).* It was a night that not only celebrated historically marginalized literary voices, but looked keenly toward what those voices mean, now more than ever. The specter of political turmoil, fear, and uncertainty about the future after a sharply divisive election hung heavy over the ceremony. But after a year when many people have looked to writers to make sense of the country's political upheaval, the National Book Awards emphasized the importance of recognizing that the stories told by people of color, and African Americans in particular, are indelible parts of the American narrative.

The prize for nonfiction, awarded to *The Atlantic's* Ta-Nehisi Coates last year, went to the historian Ibram X. Kendi for his book *Stamped From the Beginning: The Definitive History of Racist Ideas in America.* Kendi's work is a deep (and often disturbing) chronicling of how anti-black thinking has entrenched itself in the fabric of American society not solely through ignorance, but through a rationalization of inequity in institutional practices. Using the stories of five key intellectual figures—from Thomas Jefferson to Angela Davis—Kendi traces extensively, over the course of 600 pages, how history has woven racism into not just the consciousness of explicitly anti-black figures, but even the more subtly-rooted thinking of what he calls "assimilationists," a group who oppose and fight racial inequity, but find blame in both the oppressed and oppressors.

Kendi thanked his six-month old daughter Imani in his speech. Her name means "faith" in Swahili, a word that he stated has a new meaning for him now as the first black president is about to leave the White House, and a man endorsed by the Ku Klux Klan is about to enter. Kendi talked about the burden of weariness he's carried in digging through the darker chapters of American history for this book, and insisted he would keep faith in a new movement of protest against white supremacy and nationalism.

Perhaps the most eagerly-anticipated prize of the night, the award for fiction, went to Colson Whitehead, for his novel *The Underground Railroad.* The book, by an author <u>previously recognized</u> for his more fantastical work, was a heavy favorite after its <u>glowing critical reception</u>—to Whitehead's own surprise—since it was published in the summer. The story follows Cora, a slave on a cotton plantation in the antebellum South who's offered an escape via a secret network of tracks running beneath the ground. Whitehead takes a metaphor for a network of people who helped slaves escape northward, and turns it into a literal mode of salvation, as Cora moves frantically from state to state with a notorious slave-catcher hot on her heels. Accepting the award, Whitehead spoke with resolute hopefulness about what *The Underground Railroad* and the projection of black voices mean for those who must endure "the blasted hellhole wasteland of Trump-land" outside.

"Be kind to everybody, make art, and fight the power."

Whitehead wasn't the only person to reference the president-elect: The former *Nightly Show* host Larry Wilmore, who hosted the evening's proceedings, wondered how a Trump presidency might affect the book world, speculating that all copies of the constitution would effectively have to be moved to the Fiction section, and Trump's own writing re-categorized as Horror.

There are those <u>who question</u> whether or not awards like these are necessarily the means to validate or evaluate the power of literary voices, particularly when those voices are all male. The National Book Foundation—currently helmed by its first woman of color, executive director Lisa Lucas—may indeed represent a prestigious inner circle of educated elite that was effectively left flailing this election. But there was something powerful about the palpable sense of community that transcended the evening. The Literarian Award, an honorary prize presented for outstanding service to the American literary community, was given to <u>Cave Canem</u>, a nonprofit that cultivates a platform for black poets. And though Whitehead, Lewis, and Kendi all told stories explicitly dealing with notions of black racial identity in America's past, their works may be even more significant when it comes to navigating the future.

In these times of uncertainty, literature can be instructive, comforting, and inspiring. As Colson Whitehead movingly told the audience in his acceptance speech, his own advice for a Trump presidency is, "Be kind to everybody, make art, and fight the power."

7 Ways To Make A Political Statement With Books

CHARLOTTE AHLIN

The Gifted
by
Samantha Fitzgerald

You know that moment, when you lean too far back in a chair, and you have the crystal clear thought, "Oh no, I am going to fall," but it's too late to do anything about it so you fall out of the chair and smack your head anyway? Yeah. That's pretty much how I've felt since election night. I think that's probably how a *lot* of us have felt since election night. But we can't afford to lose hope, or become complacent. We need to rise up against hate and injustice. Here are a few ways that we can all make a political statement with books, starting today.

It's heartbreaking to see our country reward racism, misogyny, and demagoguery with the highest office in the land. I wish I could say that books will be enough to turn the ideological tide in America. It will take more than that, and there are many organizations out there ready to fight to preserve American's rights. Donate if you can. Volunteer if you can. Remember to breathe if you can. And in the meantime, *read.* Books may not be our sole defense, but we won't get far without them. Books have started revolutions. To everyone who's calling for national unity, and claiming that we owe the current president-elect our respect... you might want to crack open a history book (or at least listen to the *Hamilton* soundtrack). The United States of America was founded on civil disobedience and subversive writing. Let those be part of the core American values that guide us through these next four years.

So here are a few simple ways you can start to stand up and fight back through books. We can't let hate become the norm.

1. Read books written by activists

If you're at a loss for where to begin, read books by activists. Read bell hooks. Read Malala Yousafzai. Hell, read Thomas Paine if you want to, just educate yourself on the problems we're facing and the ways we can organize to solve those problems. Educate yourself on the historical factors that brought us to this moment in time. If you don't understand the opinion of someone on the other side, read books written by people you don't agree with. At the very least, you'll have more facts to lean on the next time you get into a Facebook fight with your second cousin who owns all those guns.

2. Support literacy programs

I'm not saying that every kid who has access to books grows up to be a kind, politically-aware genius... but let's try to make sure that the next generation doesn't get all their political information from memes. Organizations like Reach Out & Read and Literacy Inc. work to promote literacy in children and teens, and to provide kids with real live books. You can donate or sign up to volunteer for these or any number of other organizations dedicated to fighting illiteracy. It might not sound like a bold political stance to take, but we need well-read youth if we're going to counter the current flood of ignorance and misinformation.

3. Donate your books

I know, book lovers —your books are your darling children and it hurts to get rid of them. But the stakes are high right now (and I *know* you're not going to re-read that Stephen King paperback). There are many organizations that accept book donations for kids worldwide. And if you don't have any kids' books to donate, you can send your books to Books Through Bars or the Prison Book Program to stock prison libraries.

4. Buy and read books by marginalized authors

Yes, you should actually *buy* the books, because books that sell are books that continue to be published. Buy and read books by native writers, by transgender writers, by writers with mental illness. Whether the books are fiction, memoir, or poetry, we need diverse books now more than ever. Speaking of, you can get involved with the organization We Need Diverse Books and turn your reading habits into action.

5. Recommend what you read

Tell your friends how reading Audre Lorde has changed your life. Tell your teachers or your students about how they, too, can read more diverse books. Give your racist aunt *Invisible Man* by Ralph Ellison for Christmas. Photocopy pages from Rachel Carson's *Silent Spring* and post them all over the bulletin boards at your college. Perform your slam poem about income inequality at your coffee shop's monthly open mic. Spread radical literature every possible way you can.

6. Support independent book-sellers and publishers

It doesn't sound all that political, but supporting indie bookstores and publishers can do more than you think. You're supporting the local economy (and the local economy is about to need all the help it can possibly get). You're supporting fledgling authors, who are still building their readership. Often, you're supporting diverse authors who exist outside the mainstream media. Plus, many small-scale bookstores also operate as community centers or gathering places, and we need strong community ties if we're going to get anything done.

7. Write or support writers

Yes, we seem to be drowning in a sea of think pieces and op-eds right now. Yes, it's overwhelming. Yes, it's OK to take a break from reading rage-filled blog posts on Medium. And yes, not all of us feel comfortable putting words down on a page. But we live in a world in which the president-elect is threatening to sue the *New York Times* for criticizing him. As Orwellian as this sounds, we need to support the free press if we want it to stay free. Buy subscriptions to the newspapers that actually fact-check, because they're being drowned out by garbage-spewing websites. And, if you like your own right to free speech, use it. If you're a writer, write like hell. Write your blog posts, or your poetry, or your Great American Novel. Never doubt that your writing has the potential to add some measure of good to the world.

I Self-Published a Cookbook, Despite it All

A Guest Post by Marcy Goldman

I never wanted to self-publish. I imagined continuing Random House and Harper Collins book deals for my growing baking author platform and features in leading newspapers and online venues. I envisioned more Christmas baskets from my publishers, help with my blog and website, and publicists to set up my interviews and promotional spots.

Instead, I am now River Heart Press, my own imprint, and I am boldly going where I went when I was 12 years old and self-published my own street newspaper, *The Goldman Times*. After 25 years of great publishers, great cookbooks and what I thought was an upward spiraling career, I wasn't getting a response to my next book idea from traditional publishers. So I dove in. I self-published *When Bakers Cook*, a 276-page cookbook, in December 2013.

It has not been an easy path. I've had so much self-doubt because opinions on self-published books rest on the assumption that they are inferior simply because they are self-published. Worse, people think these books will be amateur in content and looks. This premise is applied  even if the author engages expert editors, proofreaders, formatters, and designers and thoroughly researches the distribution and promotion of the work. Without sufficient social media or platform, people assume that self-published books — even great ones — won't get noticed. I've seen a zillion blogs with this headline: "If you publish it, who will find it or you?" This suggests that Shakespeare, Dan Brown, and Elizabeth Gilbert would never have been discovered without benefit of Twitter, Facebook, or a YouTube book trailer. Do we actually believe form trumps content? No. I believe readers know a good thing when they see it.

It took three years, including wallowing in self-doubt and existential, mid-life angst about my value as a baking author, to research the self-publishing partners and players. Compared to the average text-heavy novel, self-publishing a cookbook with photos is difficult. Cookbooks require complicated book design. Our recipes need extraordinary copy editing and we also need legions of volunteer recipe testers to make sure our recipes work. On top of that, food photography, groceries and promotion often consumes a big part of the budget.

I cobbled together the budget to pay my editor, copy editor, indexer, proofreader, photographer and publishing costs with CreateSpace and Kindle. (Some of the talented staff I hired were recently let go from prestigious traditional publishers, so we can no longer assume that having a traditional book deal insures a team of editorial and sales help.)

Despite a complete manuscript, self-publishing took another 13 months. Surprisingly, while editors, agents and publishers I've worked with for years forgot to call or email me back on so many occasions, I got a call from Amazon's executive team to see how they might expedite my self-published cookbook. I got Cadillac service on my self-publishing journey for my $748 publishing package. In addition, I became an empowered employer versus a contractor.

After *When Bakers Cook* launched, the *Washington Post* named it one of the "Best Cookbooks of 2013." The book continues to sell quite nicely. It cost me about $5000 to publish a hard copy and a Kindle version. I make a nice monthly sum that, over the course of 12 months, should amount to the same as a modest cookbook advance. But my book will never go out of print, the royalties are higher, and I know daily what my earnings are, versus bi-annually when I get an advance statement in the mail. Best of all, as a self-published author, I might sell less books overall, but make disproportionately more income.

I am now at work on self-publishing another cookbook, my bestselling cookbook that went out of print, a book of food poetry, and a memoir. Why? Because I can. I am building my own back list, which will provide consistent revenue. While I respect and miss my publishers, I am no longer waiting for a publisher (or worse, the sales force or book buyer at Barnes & Noble) to ask me to create the next hot trend. No *Paleo Hanukkah Lite* cookbook for me!

During those 13 months of a horrific learning curve, as my spirits and confidence rose, I tried to share my great adventure. Few, if any colleagues, even those struggling themselves, wanted to hear. I had a sense that I've betrayed someone or crossed a line into a land I never wanted to visit. That's the part I still don't get. I'm not unique as a mid-list author. I am not unique in forging a new path, but I don't understand why authors would be so disparaging.

So if you want to publish, whether you're rife with talent or no one has dared tell you you're not, do it. If you are traditionally published and even established, but have a book your current publisher won't consider, do it. If I have to choose between a manuscript languishing in my drawer or a mediocre, inequitable, and stifling contract, <u>I will champion the self-published book.</u>

To my colleagues who dismiss or otherwise seem tepid about my efforts to stay afloat, I say jump into the pool. The water's warm and there's plenty of room.

Marcy Goldman is the host of www.betterbaking.com, celebrating its 17th year online. Her next books are The Baker's Four Seasons, Love and Ordinary Things, Poetry from the Kitchen, and the Dance Floor and Life. All her books are doing very well, in print and as e-books. She is the happiest she's ever been.

How to Leverage Tools on Amazon.com to Increase Your Sales Opportunities

A PHOTOGRAPHER'S NOTEBOOK

Photographs and Lyrical Writings from the 60's
By
Wayne H. Drumheller

A Collectible Vintage Photography Edition

Amazon.com, the world's leading online retailer, enables authors, filmmakers, and musicians to connect directly with their audience through a number of innovative features which are designed to help customers find what they are looking for. Utilize these features to encourage customers to land on your product's detail page. Below are some of the features that may lead to greater visibility on Amazon.com. Get online and explore!

Customer Reviews

Located below the editorial reviews on your product's detail page, customer reviews are opinions of other consumers who purchased your title and want to tell other shoppers what they thought.

How can this help you sell more?

Encourage anyone who tells you how much he or she enjoyed your product to write a review on Amazon.com. As your positive reviews grow, so may your sales. Don't be discouraged by the occasional less-than-glowing customer review. Having a neutral or negative review actually increases the credibility of the ratings overall, because you can't please all the people all the time (and if it looks like you are, people might be suspicious).

Rankings

Your product's sales ranking on Amazon.com can be a great selling tool to include in promotional materials. How do the rankings work? The calculation is based on Amazon.com sales and is updated each hour to reflect recent and historical sales of every item sold on the site. Sales of your title will help boost your Amazon.com sales ranking and will significantly increase your title's search relevance on Amazon.com.

So You'd Like to . . . Guides are similar to Listmania! Lists, and are a way for you to help other customers find all the items and information they might need for something they are interested in. The guides provide a great opportunity to share your advice, experiences, and product recommendations with others, and just like Listmania! Lists, you (and your friends, fans, and family) may want to create a So You'd Like to . . . Guide that features your title. It will increase the likelihood that people will come across your product while browsing on Amazon.com.

Learn how to create your own <u>So You'd Like To ... Guide</u>.

Search Inside the Book®
For authors, Amazon's Search Inside the Book program allows customers to see the interior pages of a book.

How does it work? When customers search for books, Amazon.com uses the actual words from inside participating books--not just the author, title, and keywords supplied by the publisher--to return the best possible selection of books. For matches inside the book, they also display a short excerpt and links to the page where the query matched. From any book detail page, customers have the opportunity to sample the book using the Search Inside! reader. This includes previewing sample pages, viewing a random page, or searching for a specific reference or character.

Titles submitted to the Search Inside the Book program are automatically eligible for personalization and merchandising features throughout Amazon.com, such as recommendations. With this helpful search feature, customers can discover books that may never have surfaced in previous search results.

All CreateSpace titles are submitted for the Search Inside the Book program, free of charge.

Take advantage of the many tools Amazon.com offers and your title may become the next great thing customers didn't even know they were looking for!

Looking for more helpful information and advice? Check out our <u>Resources</u>, <u>Community</u>, and <u>Help</u> sections.

Permalink: <u>http://www.createspace.com/resources/sell_more</u>

About Book Marketing Agencies!

Google News

Want do we think we really know? Get a glimpse into the philosophy, ideology and leadership style that makes book publicity agency thrive or die in the industry.

As in any industry, companies come and go, and this is certainly true with book promotion companies. Perhaps more than most, book publicity is a fiercely competitive niche industry in which book PR services and book publicity firms that don't evolve with industry changes inevitably perish. More than 70% of the book PR agencies, book promoters, and one-person shops have closed their doors recently.

TOP BOOK TIPS & ADVICE

- How to Market Your Book
- 110 Book Marketing Ideas to Promote Your Book
- 15 Top FAQ's about Book Marketing
- Book Marketing Resources for Authors
- The Ultimate Guide to a Successful Book Marketing Plan
- Proven Methods to Market Your Business Book
- Questions to Ask Your Book Marketing Agency
- Self Published Book Marketing
- Non Fiction Book Marketing

How to Sell Your Self-Published Book to Bookstores

Author unknown

In the past, getting independent booksellers to shelve self-published books was a difficult prospect. Indie booksellers were reluctant to sell self-published books, based on the <u>old bias</u> that self-published meant poor content or poor quality. But that was then and this is now. Not only have self-published authors upped their game when it comes to content, but the quality of self-published books is highly competitive with those of traditionally published books. So just how do you go about selling your book to independent bookstores?

Much as writing books is a passion and business for authors, selling books is a passion and the *only* business for independent booksellers. And while independent bookstores are known for being wonderful community gathering places with staff that genuinely care about the book industry, that doesn't mean they can do it all for the love. They still need to sell books. Everyone has to make a living in this business, and this is what the independent booksellers need for you and your book in order for both you and them to succeed in selling it.

Know Your Audience

1. Booksellers do not want to hear about your success at Amazon.com!

It's great to have success on <u>Amazon</u>, whether as a traditionally published author or self-published author, but consider the fact that indie bookstores have to compete with them before you brag about how well your book is selling there; it won't help you get your book in your local independent bookstore. In fact, Amazon is their biggest competitor, which is one way IngramSpark's self-publishing platform is uniquely positioned to help indie authors achieve more success in this particular retail market. Independent booksellers reject stocking books published via <u>Amazon KDP</u>, because their sales of those titles ultimately profits their biggest competitor.

2. Be a good customer.

Don't just know a store exists via Google searches. Actually know them. Cultivate relationships with indie booksellers by purchasing books from their stores and encouraging your friends, family, and fans to do so as well. It makes sense to support your local independent bookstore before you ask them to support you. It's one way to be a good literary citizen—and it's good business, too.

Independent bookstores have become more than just a place to buy a book; they are constantly evolving. Indie bookstores are community hotspots—supporting the local community, creating publishing programs, publishing and selling their own unique content, and hosting author events. When pitching your book to an indie bookseller, consider the unique ways your book ties into supporting the bookstore and the community. Your support of them will make them more likely to support you.

Before you approach a bookstore owner, research his or her background. Get a feel for the shop's customers and the types of books the store typically promotes and sells. Take a look at the store's social media accounts and see what kinds of author events they typically host. When you meet with the owner, use this information in your pitch. If they have a certain type of customer that will be interested in your book, mention it.

3. Know a store's demographic.

A bookstore owner wants to make sure your book aligns with their customers. Niche bookstores may only carry a certain genre. Know your genre and your target reader. Be able to accurately and concisely explain what your book is about. That way, you and the bookstore will have a better idea if it fits with their readership.

Spend enough time at the store you're targeting to understand who their customers are. Their readers won't be your readers if your readers don't shop at that kind of bookstore. Familiarize yourself with their inventory and see if your book fits in. If an indie bookseller does not foresee his/her customers buying your book from their store, he/she is not going to buy it from you.

Discounted and Returnable

If you want your book to flow easily into independent bookstores, then consider the 55% wholesale discount and make it returnable. The book industry is a returnable industry, which means bookstores will expect to be able to return books they don't sell and get a credit for their return.

Keep in mind that a bookstore is not likely to buy numerous copies from you outright. They want to be sure your book will sell before they take on more than one or two copies. If you're self-published, print-on-demand services are a cost-effective way to get your book out there. A bookstore will be more likely to buy your book if the distributor has return capabilities, such as IngramSpark's, and if you set bookstore-friendly terms regarding the wholesale discount. Beyond the fact that it's run by their competition, bookstores don't generally take Amazon KDP publications because they don't allow returns.

Quality Product

Bookstores want to be about 90% sure that they can sell a book before they buy it, so that means that you have to give the bookstore a quality product. Something that stands out qualitatively and fits in beautifully genre-wise.

Easily Shelved

Your book needs to be easily shelved by the bookstore. Booksellers don't want something that looks or sounds so unusual that no one knows where to put it. So if you have the idea that your book is completely unique and there is nothing like it out there in the universe, you need to visit a lot of stores and libraries and go online and figure out what people will be looking for when they discover your book.

It's one of your jobs as a self-publisher to figure out <u>how people will actually discover your book</u>, and if your book is labeled or packaged so uniquely that the bookstore doesn't know where to put it on the shelf, then you're just creating difficulty for yourself. Booksellers aren't interested in books that stick out for the wrong reasons. Visit your local bookstore and take note of the <u>trim sizes</u>, <u>book cover imagery</u>, and <u>interiors</u>. Your book doesn't need to look like a clone of everyone else's, but if you notice themes for certain genres, stick with that, because they most likely represent industry standards for a particular genre that shouldn't be tinkered with.

Appropriate Retail Price

Make sure your book has an <u>appropriate retail price</u>. There are some books that are more manuals and textbooks where you won't be printing very many or there is such a specific demand for them they're what some people call a destination book and you can charge a premium price for them. There are others that might be more mind candy or fluff or impulse buy and those would have a lower price. This is where your market research comes in. You want your book to fit into its category and stand out qualitatively so that the end buyer doesn't end up with sticker shock. "Oh, all these other textbooks are $48.95 and here's one that's $9.95. Huh, it might not be very good." Make sure you do your research to find out with which titles yours could most closely be compared.

Easy Ordering

Having your book available via IngramSpark will be of great comfort to booksellers. Ingram is well-respected within the book industry and a reliable resource to booksellers when it comes to someone supplying them with books.

A bookseller won't want to deal with inconvenient distribution. When they work with distributors, they can order, sell, and invoice books in bulk. But working with indie authors means they have to do all of this individually with each author. Using a reputable distributor for your book will be more convenient for the bookstore, and the easier you make it for an indie bookstore to sell your book, the more likely they are to be willing to try.

Publisher/Author Support on the Book Sale

What booksellers are looking for is what kind of publisher/author support they're going to get from you for the sell through. There are thousands of stores and outlets in this country, so what is going to draw an individual to a particular store to look for your particular book?

It's the bookstore's job to sell your book, not market it. Busy bookstores may be approached by authors often, and they are inundated with consignment offers on any given day. You will be expected to fulfill your end of the bargain in the form of marketing. The bookstore wants your book to sell, but don't expect the store to do the legwork for you. Have a solid marketing plan in place, and let the bookstore owner know what it is. It will show them that you take initiative and have confidence that your book will sell.

If you want your book to sell at a specific store, start a grassroots book marketing campaign to make it happen. Have your friends and family who live and/or shop near the store request copies of your book. Have them stagger their requests so your book establishes a consistent sales record. When you approach that store to ask if they'll stock your book, management will be more likely to say, "Yes!" if they've already sold some copies of it.

Market Indie Bound as a Way Consumers Can Buy Your Book

Your author website, advertising, and marketing materials may direct readers to Amazon.com and Barnes & Noble, but you should also include IndieBound.org. IndieBound supports sales through local bookstores by linking purchasers of your book to independent bookstores in their area. It's important that you represent IndieBound alongside other retail outlets. By giving readers the opportunity to choose to purchase from an indie bookstore, you are showing local booksellers that you are a savvy author and that you actively encourage sales of your book from independent bookstores.

You might have more luck locally and regionally. Some local indie bookstores will just want to buy from you on a consignment basis because that might be easier for them. Some of them might want to do an event first to test the waters. But ultimately booksellers want to know what kind of buzz you're going to generate to help achieve the sell through. Think of bookstores like restaurants. If you owned a small restaurant you'd have to keep turning those tables during your dinner service so that you could make enough money to keep your doors open. Much like you can't just have one customer take up a table for hours on end, you also can't just park a book in a bookstore. You need to not only help it get onto the shelves with the tips above, but you also need to help it get back off them and in the arms of a paying bookstore customer.

11 Powerful Book Promotion Ideas for Self-Published Authors

From Bookeditage.com

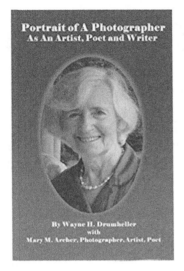

If you write only because you love to, you won't need to bother with marketing. But if you are publishing by yourself and wish to be read by as many among your target audience as possible, you will have to learn an additional skill—how to market your books. It would help to be clear about your goals at the outset, because effective book marketing takes some early planning and effort.

For authors, marketing essentially involves drawing and engaging your target audience by sharing more about yourself and your book. It really is as simple as communicating. But it involves work. In this article, we share 11 book promotion ideas that will improve your book's visibility among your target audience and help you sell more books. Some of the suggestions, like entering metadata, are inherent to a book's publishing process and would require little additional effort. Some other ways to market suggested here may appear unnecessary; but remember your goals, and exercise the same discipline with your book marketing plan as you would in your writing.

1. Have your own blog or website

You can help potential readers find you even before you finish writing your book. Update your site with articles that would surface in your target audience's organic search results. For example, if your book is about managing emotional well-being, cover the latest scientific developments in the field, and intersperse them with insights from your book. If your book is a work of fiction, you could review the most popular books or memorable characters in the genre.

As you come close to the launch date, you can create buzz around your book through contests and book giveaways. Post high-quality content that encourages your target audience to subscribe for updates. If your site has about a year's lead over your book's launch date, it will give you time to build a substantial mailing list and improve your site's ranking.

2. Increase your online presence to spread the word about your book

There are several ways in which you can increase your online presence. For example, you can post your articles on popular websites that receive a lot of traffic, or contribute on forums that discuss topics related to your book, or request websites or blogs that are popular among your target audience to feature you in an interview or guest post.

In your byline, remember to include a link to your website and the books you have written or are presently writing.

3. Use social media

Set up an author page on Facebook and an account with Twitter. Observe what kind of posts and promotions get the most likes, shares, and retweets, and apply the insights to increase your social media following and engage with them better.

4. Learn from the most popular books in your genre — what helps them sell?

Examining their titles, cover designs, and typography will show you what works in your genre. Shortlist the ones that you like best or do not like at all, and think through your reasons for each inference.

There are more benefits to studying the best books. As you read their reviews, you will come across words and phrases that connect with and characterize your target audience. By including these in descriptions for your book's metadata, you can help your book be discovered by your target audience through their search queries.

As you go about this process, keep your eyes open for balanced and insightful reviews; you can add the reviewers to your shortlist and approach them for a review when your book is ready.

5. Get reviews for your book

One of the quickest ways to get reviews for your new book is to approach reviewers of any of your previous books with a free copy and a polite request.

If you are a first-time author, you could look up Amazon's top reviewers and shortlist the ones who have reviewed books from your genre.

While Amazon does not support reviews for pre-order books, if you have released a paperback version of your book and linked it to your unreleased ebook, any reviews posted for the paperback will copy over to your ebook. This way, your book will be ready with social proof right from the day it is launched.

You can also promote your pre-release book among Goodread's network of over 65 million members through a featured giveaway. Goodreads allows reviews to be posted for pre-release books. Take note that even though Amazon owns Goodreads, reviews posted on one site cannot be migrated to the other.

As a rule of thumb, contact four times as many reviewers as the number of reviews you are aiming for. Follow up at least once, preferably a week or two after your first email.

You should also approach influential book bloggers, popular authors in your genre, and newspapers for editorial reviews.

6. Write an enticing book blurb

A book blurb is a short promotional piece of about 100–150 words. It appears on the back cover of print books and on online sales pages.

To write an effective blurb, begin with a clever opening line that piques the reader's curiosity and has them reading for more. Follow that up with a hint about your plot and characters (for fiction) or the core concept (for nonfiction), using compelling words such as *amazing, incredible, mysterious, powerful, life-altering*—depending on your book's genre.

The closing should grip your reader. For fiction, you could present a crossroads or turning point in the story; for nonfiction, you could mention who should read the book and why.

If your book has received any editorial reviews, add them to the blurb.

7. Invest in a professional cover design service

Would anyone spare a second glance for a book whose cover is too busy, has jarring colors and typeface, or looks unpolished and unprofessional? A well-designed cover is crucial to a book's salability, and this is better achieved by using a professional book cover design service.

8. Maximize your distribution channels

Amazon is the biggest retailer of digital and print books and owns 2 self-publishing service companies—Kindle Direct Publishing (KDP) for ebooks and CreateSpace for print books. If you include Amazon's KDP, Apple's iBooks, Barnes & Noble's Nook, and Kobo in your distribution plan, you would have covered the channels that account for 97% of ebook sales. Smaller retailers account for a negligible proportion of sales, but they help to increase visibility.

If you do not want to deal with individual companies, you can publish with an ebook aggregator such as *Smashwords or Draft2Digital. Ebook aggregators distribute to multiple retailers and format books to the requirements of each. They also give access to channels that authors cannot approach directly, such as Scribd, a digital library with a subscription service used by 80 million people worldwide.

9. Make the most of Amazon's book promotional tools and programs

Amazon has a formidable range of promotional tools and programs that you should put to good use.

KDP Select: To enroll into this program, you must give Amazon exclusive distribution rights to your ebook for a 90-day period. Discounting is known to be very effective in improving visibility and sales, and for any five days during this period, you can offer your book for free or set up a countdown deal. Moreover, any book sales generated under this program will fetch you Amazon's highest royalty rate of 70%.

KDP Select would also enter your book into Kindle Unlimited, a subscription service that helps subscribers discover and read books, and pays authors depending on the number of pages read.

If KDP Select works well for you, you can re-enroll into the program as many times as you want.

Amazon Author Central: By setting up an Author Central account, you can have your own page on Amazon, with your biography, photos, videos, events, and details of every book you have published. This page also attaches to the sales pages of all the books you are selling on Amazon. You can personalize the contents of your page and even share its URL on your social media sites and in your email signature to drive more traffic to it.

<u>Expanded Distribution Program</u>: This program offers authors the opportunity to make their print books available at various online retailers and physical bookstores, libraries, and academic institutions in the United States. If you enroll into this <u>program</u>, your book will be listed in the catalogs of distributors and can be ordered by sellers and libraries connected to the distributors' ordering systems.

10. Use book discounting sites like Bookbub and Book Gorilla

Bookbub and Book Gorilla are book recommendation services whose subscribers receive a daily email, recommending titles from book genres or authors they have professed interest in. In order to be recommended, you will have to offer your book for free or at a minimum discount of 50% for a limited period.

While some services offer free book promotion, most of the good ones charge a fee, which depends on the price and genre of the book. For <u>Bookbub's hottest category</u> of crime fiction, the listing fee is about $400 for books being offered for free, and about $2000 for books being sold in the price range of $2–$3.

Bookbub's growing popularity among authors, as understood from online reviews and message boards, tells us that book promotions do indeed drive sales above pre-promotion levels, even after the promotion is over. The benefits apply not only to the book being promoted but also to other books written by the author. Authors have also observed that promotions are followed by a spike in book reviews.

11. Join the **Goodreads Author Program**

Goodreads' network of over 65 million members makes it a useful promotional platform. You can create your own profile page to share about yourself and your books, seek reviews, organize book giveaways, host discussions regarding your books, add your books to the appropriate lists on <u>Listopia</u> where they can be seen and voted for by your target audience, and more!

Summary

Strategizing about book marketing holds little importance for authors going through a <u>traditional book publisher</u>. The publisher will take care of book marketing and distribution, including arranging for editorial reviews, book launch and signing events, a spot in a book fair, featured articles in newspapers, and a place in bookstores. Self-publishing authors, on the other hand, have to figure these things out for themselves, drawing advice and inspiration from as many sources as possible.

This article does not intend to provide an exhaustive list of book marketing ideas. Rather, its purpose is to help you understand that at its core, marketing is communicating about your book and making it available on as many platforms as possible. As you get started on the book marketing tips offered here, you will come across many more ways to promote your book and reach more readers. One thing will lead to another. The key is to get started. Happy marketing!

You're Invited: Free "Writing as Art, Publishing & Publicizing" Workshop by Zoom call.

You are invited to a Free "Writing as Art, Publishing & Publicizing" workshop by ZOOM on Monday, February 15th from 10:00–11:30 am.

Confirmation by Friday, February 13th via return email to waynedrumheller.hd@gmail.com is required. Materials for the workshop will be sent as confirmations are received.

On or by Sunday, February 14th all respondents will receive a zoom link for the workshop.

This zoom workshop will cover the 'pages, phases and stages' of writing a book. Participants will receive a checklist for success worksheet for writing and publishing a book along with a hands-on survey worksheet for use during the workshop. Participants will also be invited to discuss their books and best practices for publicizing and selling books.

The seminar is free, but participants should confirm attendance by contacting: waynedrumheller.hd@gmail.com for the event. The seminar is self-funded by the Creative Short Book Writers Project which funds one free seminar or workshop a month in different communities in the Carolinas and Virginia. Participants will learn about "Looking to the Future" a full-length book, with 35-40 personal interviews and stories, to be published about the past, present and future of the Alamance County, North Carolina textile industry.

On a personal note, Wayne is Editor and Founder of the Creative Short Book Writers Project, a mutually beneficial collective of independently, published authors, book editors, teachers, educators, artisans and everyday people who commit to professionally edit and publish books. He is a Burlington, North Carolina based photojournalist and Writer-In-Residence for the Textile Heritage Museum, Glencoe, NC. He is also the author of 15 fiction and non-fiction books. He received his Bachelor's Degree from Sonoma State University, California and Masters of Education from the University of North Carolina at Greensboro. He is a member of the Burlington Writers Club, Virginia Blue Ridge Writers Club, Rockfish River Valley Writers, North Carolina Writers' Network and a series of independent writers and photographers' groups across the USA.

My latest book *"1000 People of Meaning and Purpose"* is available to buy at www. Amazon.com/books.

Wayne Drumheller
Photojournalist, Published Author, Book Editor, Publicist
Burlington, NC 27215

Phone/Text: 336-266-6461
Email: waynedrumheller.hd@gmail.com   www.waynedrumheller.com

Zoom is a great tool for gathering writers and published authors to review and talk about best practices, publicity and selling published book. Join my zoom calls any time you can and learn more about writing and publishing independently on KDP.amazon.com.

A Special Thank You to those who have participated in my "Writing as Art, Editing & Publishing" workshops since 2010.

I am grateful to the following people for attending, participating and publishing your books, through my 'Writing as Art, Editing & Publishing" or "Published! Now What?" workshops since I became Editor and Founder of the Short Book Writers Project in 2010:

Georgia Ahalt, Donna Allen, Linda P. Angel, Mary M. Archer, Ian Baltutis, Kevin Blackford, Kathy Bonham, Faye Boswell, Kathryn Stripling Byer, Shirley Cadmus, Beth Canada, Doris Caruso, Sondra Casey, Debra Chandler, Bill and Marianna Clarke, Nancy Clark, Sandy W. Clarke, Roger Lee Coburn, Lynn Coffey, Bobby Collier, Pattie Apple Cook, Anna Florence Crawford, Glenn Crossman, Carol Cutler, Ph.D., Margaret Dardess, Ph.D., Lucy Daniels, Melanie Dellinger, Joan and Doris DeMastus, Karon Dewey, Ph.D., Edward Di Gangi, Kathy Dillon, Will & Joan Dinkins, Rev. Bob Disher, Patti Donahue, Dr. Don Dressler, Edward and Jodie Drumheller, Malcolm Drumheller, Gary and Amy Drumheller, Sara Edmond, Fran Barry Edwards, Carl Eggleston, Margarita Escaler, Ph.D., Bettie Farmer, Dabney E. Farmer, Melinda Fargis, Joshua Fitzgerald, Wayne and Jimmy Fortune, Mary Flytle, Cliff and Evelyn Frady, Dan Fuhrman, Wesley Buell Frazier, Cherie Garland, Gare Galbraith, Steve Gaultney, Sandy Goble, Doug and Sonja Gorsline, Hope Christmas Goude, Sarah Green, Tim Green, Carolyn Grinnell, Dr. Charles Hamner, Earl Hamner Jr., Kristy Ward Haney, Joe Harman, Mayor Jimmy Harris, Lane Hash, Norma Green Heath, Teresa Higgins, Roy and Nan Hill, Susan Huffman, Irene Hughes, Julia Clarke Huneycutt, Carolyn Ives, Phel Jacobson, Elaine Jones, Sarah Julen, Lonnie Kantor, Kathryn Keck, Kathy Kiehl. Nick Kinney, Walter Kluge, Marie Koury, Kristy Kraft, Gerry Kruger, Lucy W. Kernodle, Debbie Layman, Evelyn Leathers, Ph. D., Robert, Ben, Tim and Kelly Locklear, Chuck Lumpkin, Al Manning, Katie Marie, Tamra Marshall, Beverley Martin, Lucy Ewing Martin, Cara Mayo, David McCoy, Aubrey McClain, Shirley Miller, Florine Moize, Alice Bryant Moore, Tanya Renee Moore, Morgan Moore, Barbara Morris, Rita Odom Moseley, Delores Ann Hughes McGann, David Munson, George T. Nall, Joe Namath, George and Jerrie Nall, JZ Noyes, Miriam Pace, Janet Paduhovich, Ron and Linda Padgett, Marisa Panzer, Mike Papadaes, Avice Parker, Susan N. Parker, Mike and Beth Parry, Darryl Pebbles, Janice Penxa, Lori H. Ponton, Dr. Sam Powell, Lynn Pownell, Ron Petree, Nancy Purcell, Clara Roberts, Robert Roberts, Jean Bailey Robor, Jamie Rollins, Elaine Ruggieri, Carol Rullman, Larry Sabato, Janet Sady, Paul Saunders, Max Shephard, Millie Phillips Shaffer, Shirley Sanders, Kathryn Scarborough, Orin Shepherd, Joe Sledge, Frances Smith, Devon Smith, Bonnie McKinney Stevens, Olivia Lee Stogner, Craig Stewart, Fred Strawson, Marilyn and Jimmie Stein, Laurie Smith, Vicki and Earl Smith, Brian W Spangler, Nina Spear, Michelle Monroe Spurlock, Jean Spurgill, Elizabeth Solazzo, Sara Skowron, Norm and Margarite Sowards, Charles P. Stanley, Aleen Steinberg, Tim and Susie Summers, Lisa Swinson, Molly and Tom Tartt, Carol Jean Taylor, Jim and Carolyn Teague, Richard Thomas, Marta Anne Tice, Carole Watterson Troxler, Ph.D., Bill Tucker, Jeannie Uchno, J. E. Van Horn, M.D., William Woody Vick, Mile and Barbara Vipperman, Donna D. Vitucci, Tanae Walker, William Wallace, Mary Baker Ware, Joanne Whatley, Lisa Watlington, Jenifer Webb, Rod Webb, Christine Wethman, Doris White, Michelle White, Daisy Valladares Whited, Jerry Whitmire, Thomas

Whitmire, Jackie Whitmire, Gaye Frances Willard, Jay and Penny Williams, Mamie Marie Willis, Brenda Loy Wilson, Charlie Wilson, Lori Welch Wilson, Corinna Workman, Charlie Zeiglar, Roxanne Zusmer and many others.

New additions as of January 1, 2022

Mike Auen, Charles Chip Dull, Megan Furr, Becky Howard, Elder John Jeffries, Linda Greenwood, Robert Frank Hensley, Vondra Jones, Lisa Russel Dulvernay, Melissa R. Smith, Dean and Starr Jones, Charlie Hughes, Richard Lacy Duck, Master Sergeant Joseph J. Lipkowicz, Judy Madren, Mary Montgomery, Norman and Marie Napier, Donna Boslett Roach, Mary Speight, Scotti Stover Troxell, John P. Vavalee, MD, Patricia Duck, Jeffries Wharton, Kimberly Russel Williams

New additions as of January 1, 2023

The Lisa and Brian Cardosa Family, Bennie Dodd, Jimmy Fortune, Steve and Dee Fox, James Lester Fortune Jr., Doris Truslow Drumheller, Jennifer H. Durkee, Dee and Steve Fox, Pameka Franklin Hall, Mary Buford Hitz, Diane Hitzke, Pamela Franlin Hall, K. Kay Lay. Ph. D., Tom Jones, Ph.D., Astronaut, Professor K. Edward Lay, Bob RB Martin, Frank Pappa Napier, Linda Patrick Nicholas, Richard Parker, The Nick Poirier Family, Matthew Pippin, Mary Jo Russell, Marshall Saunders, Pat Echolyn Saunders, Bennett Saunders, The Sara and Chris Tice Family, Mike Timberlake, Cheryl Wilder, Dr. Beverly Willis,

New additions as of January 1, 2024 Jackie Campbell Clark, Johnnie Richmond, Linda Reville, Robert and Pat Saunders, Wade Lanning, Pamela Hall, Dr James Brewer, Colonel Larry D. Huffman, USMC (Ret), Andrea Chase, Connie Holt, Sheila Brooks, Dorsey and Britaney Kordich, Sheila M. Brooks, Jackie Campbell, Clark, Anna Minott, Dr. Dave Olson, Iva Knapp, Patricia Redmon, Linda Branch

Last Advice about Self-Publishing

Mike Buchanan is a self-publisher selling books through his imprint LPS publishing. He's been published and he's self-published, and much prefers the latter. In 2010, at the age of 52, he took early retirement to focus full-time on writing and self-publishing.

He's self-published six non-fiction titles since 2008 including The Joy of Self-Publishing. 'You want to be a writer?' my father said. 'My dear boy, have some consideration for your poor wife. You'll be sitting around the house all day, wearing a dressing-gown, brewing tea, and stumped for words.' John Mortimer 1923-2009 English novelist, barrister and dramatist: Clinging to the Wreckage (1982)

If you're interested in having your books published but you've been unable to interest a literary agent or publisher in your work, you're in good company. The overwhelming majority of previously unpublished writers struggle to interest literary agents or commercial publishers in their work, and the challenge is becoming more difficult with each passing year.

The tried and tested solution to this problem? Embrace self-publishing until such time as the literary world recognizes your genius. The list of writers who launched their careers by self-publishing is a long one: it includes Percy Bysshe Shelley, Walt Whitman, Virginia Woolf, John Galsworthy, Rudyard Kipling, Beatrix Potter, Lord Byron, Mark Twain, DH Lawrence, James Joyce, Robbie Burns… and many bestselling writers in the modern era including Stephen King and Bill Bryson.

By self-publishing you'll be following a noble tradition; and the good news it that it's never been more feasible to self-publish and distribute your books to buyers worldwide at minimal cost.

As you're a visitor to The Writers' Workshop website I can assume you're serious about your writing; as a reader of this article I assume you have a potential interest in having your books self-published with high production standards, comparable with books published by leading commercial publishers. There is no need for a self-published book to appear self-published. Mike Buchanan is author of The Joy of Self-Publishing.

ABOUT THE AUTHOR AND THIS BOOK

Wayne Drumheller is a Virginia native and Burlington, North Carolina based photojournalist, writing consultant, book editor and photographer. He started a second full-time career as editor and founder for the Creative Short Book Writers' Project in 2010.

Editing and producing illustrated books by aspiring artisan writers and illustrators has become his passion. Through a partial gifts-in-kind-support for book cover design, title page and copyright setup, page formatting and content printing, he offers free monthly workshops to interested authors and writers groups in communities in the Carolinas and Virginia.

Since 2010, he has helped over 200 regional writers independently publish their autobiographies, biographies, children's literature books, memoirs, collections of prose/poetry and full length nonfiction historical novels. All net proceeds from his consulting and editing workshops, books, photographs, illustrations and cover designs go to the Creative Short Book Writers Project. His fine photography work is recognized by collectors for his unique creative approach and commitment to the finished print. Many of his original photographs are in private homes in Virginia, North Carolina, New York, Florida and California.

With his grandsons' Cole and Jake in Denali National Park, Alaska 2017

His photographs have been published in his books: available at amazon.com.

Wayne's Amazing Apple Recipe Book
Wayne's Awesome Recipe Book and The American Revolution in Virginia Portrait of A Photographer as a Writer, Poet and Publisher, 1963 to Now
1000 Everyday People of Meaning and Purpose
100 Books I've Helped Publish You Should Read But Probably Never Will
Appalachian Sunrise: Finding My Way Home,
Blue Mountain Highway Home,
A Rockfish Valley Poet and His Camera,
A Rockfish Valley Photographer and his Poetry
A Photographer's Notebook: From the 1960's.
A Photographer's Notebooks: My Journey Into Everyday Life
My Alamance: A Photographer's Notebook,
Fifty Over Sixty, Finding Meaning and Purpose
Looking to the Future of the Heritage Textile Museum
Looking to the Future of Old Winter Green, Virginia

Bringing Our Family History To Life in Old Winter Green, Virginia
Old Winter Days, Stories, Tales, & Poetry, Nelson County, VA.
Light in the Dark, A Photographer's Story & Portfolio
Selected Writings from the Heart of Alamance County
Living Above The Waterfalls: A Photographer's Notebook
Our Rockfish Valley People and Their Stories
Writing As Art, Editing & Publishing
Published! Now What?

His advanced education in photography, photojournalism and writing began at seventeen when he left his home near Wintergreen, Virginia to serve in the US Army. As a photographer and student of the history of photography, he learned early that he could create, reflect and even mirror the simple things in life and celebrate the goodness to be found in most people.

He received his Bachelor's Degree from Sonoma State University, California and his Master of Education from the University of North Carolina at Greensboro. He is an active member of the Blue Ridge Writers' Club of Virginia, North Carolina Writers' Network, Burlington Writers Club, Rockfish River Valley Fine Arts Gallery, Alamance Photography Club, Burlington Artists League Gallery and the Photography Society of America.

He is the Host and Founder of monthly book presentations, signing and selling venue opportunities such as; the "Alamance County Writers' Night" in Burlington, North Carolina and "Caswell County Writers Night in Yanceyville, North Carolina and "Rockfish River Valley Writers Night" in Nelson County, Nellysford, Virginia. .

He can also be contacted at:
waynedrumheller.hd@gmail.com
wd2999@yahoo.com
Facebook.com/waynedrumheller
Burlingtonartistsleague.com/events
Alamanceartisans.org

.

Made in the USA
Middletown, DE
08 January 2025

68721401R00077